"In this work, Juan Pablo Lucchelli succeeds in explaining one of the most complex subjects in Jacques Lacan's body of work, the objet a. Lucchelli renders with breathtaking clarity the basic paradox of objet a: it is an object which is ultimately just a place-holder of the void of desire, an object with no proper place which just curves the space of desire, making a detour more efficient than a direct approach. This is a book that should not be missing not only from any library devoted to Lacan but also from the library of anyone who is perplexed by his/her desire."

Slavoj Žižek, author, *How to Read Lacan*

Understanding Lacan's Objet a

Understanding Lacan's Objet a proposes that we modify the accepted approach to Lacan's ideas and strive to make Lacanian concepts accessible.

Juan Pablo Lucchelli gradually introduces conceptual tools, following the emergence of this 'object of objects' step by step. The book makes clear the impact of the social in the genesis of objet a as a concept, with the inevitable sharing of the subject's being with others at its core. Lucchelli demonstrates that there can be no true autonomy of the individual without recognizing the dependence on the other; thus, like Winnicott's transitional object, Lacan's objet a is what connects us to others, despite the individualistic pretensions that emerge from the ego.

This book will be essential reading both for Lacanian analysts in practice and in training, who wish to deepen their knowledge of the concept of the objet a, and for students of psychoanalysis, philosophy and psychology.

Juan Pablo Lucchelli is a psychiatrist and psychoanalyst in Switzerland. He is a member of the École de la cause freudienne (Paris), a published author, and the Head Doctor for the Mental Health Unit of the Swiss Medical Network.

The Lines of the Symbolic in Psychoanalysis Series
Series Editor: Ian Parker
Manchester Psychoanalytic Matrix

Psychoanalytic clinical and theoretical work is always embedded in specific linguistic and cultural contexts and carries their traces, traces which this series attends to in its focus on multiple contradictory and antagonistic 'lines of the Symbolic'. This series takes its cue from Lacan's psychoanalytic work on three registers of human experience, the Symbolic, the Imaginary and the Real, and employs this distinctive understanding of cultural, communication and embodiment to link with other traditions of cultural, clinical and theoretical practice beyond the Lacanian symbolic universe. The Lines of the Symbolic in Psychoanalysis Series provides a reflexive reworking of theoretical and practical issues, translating psychoanalytic writing from different contexts, grounding that work in the specific histories and politics that provide the conditions of possibility for its descriptions and interventions to function. The series makes connections between different cultural and disciplinary sites in which psychoanalysis operates, questioning the idea that there could be one single correct reading and application of Lacan. Its authors trace their own path, their own line through the Symbolic, situating psychoanalysis in relation to debates which intersect with Lacanian work, explicating it, extending it and challenging it.

Queer Theory, Lacanian Psychoanalysis, Sexual Politics
From Norm to Desire
Luiz Valle Junior

Taking Back Desire
A Psychoanalytic Approach to Queerness and Neoliberalism on Screen
James Lawrence Slattery

Understanding Lacan's Objet a
Juan Pablo Lucchelli

For more information about the series, please visit: https://www.routledge.com/The-Lines-of-the-Symbolic-in-Psychoanalysis-Series/book-series/KARNLOS

Understanding Lacan's Objet a

Juan Pablo Lucchelli

Routledge
Taylor & Francis Group

LONDON AND NEW YORK

British Library Cataloguing-in-Publication Data
A catalogue record for this book is available from the British Library

ISBN: 978-1-041-01332-7 (hbk)
ISBN: 978-1-041-01331-0 (pbk)
ISBN: 978-1-003-61420-3 (ebk)

DOI: 10.4324/9781003614203

Typeset in Times New Roman
by Apex CoVantage, LLC

For Emily

Contents

Preface

It is normally demanded of any kind of introduction to a concept, including psychoanalytic concepts, that a clear definition be given at the outset, yet Juan Pablo Lucchelli, in this faithful reading of what Lacan was proud to have called his "invention" of the objet petit a, defies that demand and expectation. We learn, in this detailed scholarly book about a crucial concept in Lacanian psychoanalysis, that a "definition" would betray what is so decidedly and ineluctably ambiguous and insubstantial about this peculiar object.

This refusal has consequences for clinical and theoretical work in psychoanalysis and for how we approach the embedded nature of psychoanalysis in contemporary subjectivity, and also for our analysis of the cultural-historical conditions in which psychoanalysis is able to open up what it is to be a subject. This kind of subject is intertwined with a form of anxiety that is, Lacan notes, "not without an object." The objet petit a is an alluring object that seems to be at the core of our being, and at the core of the being of others to whom we are linked, linking together the symbolic, the imaginary and the real. What we are as a subject is inextricably bound up with what we are for others; what we are in the social field, the symbolic, what we think we are for others, the imaginary, and what always remains of the symbolic and the imaginary, what is ineliminable about who we are, the real.

This book shows us that an introduction that resists "definition" of its object of study, an "understanding" that resists "imaginarisation," necessarily requires a series of detours into a number of other phenomena, including of anxiety and jouissance, of lack and even into the relationship between Lacan and Marx as we explore reification and commodity fetishism. Here is a different way of approaching what is sometimes mistakenly, misleadingly termed an understanding of the individual in "social context."

The objet petit a is at the crux of our work on the symbolic, the imaginary and the real, there as the hinge-point, centre of the diagram Lacan gives us late on in his work, of the "Borromean Knot;" it is there at the intersection of the three circles representing the three orders of being, the three interdependent registers that we use to orient our analysis. This object is there at the centre, itself unrepresentable. It is unrepresentable as such, but its effects can be traced, with this book revealing it as the beating heart of Lacanian psychoanalysis.

Psychoanalytic clinical and theoretical work circulates through multiple inter-secting antagonistic symbolic universes. This series opens connections between different cultural sites in which Lacanian work has developed in distinctive ways, in forms of work that question the idea that there could be single correct reading and application. The Lines of the Symbolic in Psychoanalysis series provides a reflexive reworking of psychoanalysis that transmits Lacanian writing from around the world, steering a course between the temptations of a metalanguage and imagi-nary reduction, between the claim to provide a god's eye view of psychoanalysis and the idea that psychoanalysis must everywhere be the same. And the elaboration of psychoanalysis in the symbolic here grounds its theory and practice in the his-tory and politics of the work in a variety of interventions that touch the real.

Ian Parker
Manchester Psychoanalytic Matrix

Introduction

What is the object a? It would be tempting to say that the question is poorly framed and that the object a is not something that can be defined unequivocally. The text you are about to read proposes that we modify the usual way of approaching Lacan's ideas, and it strives to make Lacanian concepts as clear as possible. Above all, it seeks to reduce as much as possible the referential opacity to which so many psychoanalytic authors have accustomed us. Moreover, we will try to resort as little as possible to terms as ambiguous as object, desire, jouissance, phallus, signifier, subject, fantasy, and so on. It is not that we should avoid exploring these terms, but rather, that we should aim to use them properly by putting them to the test, beyond merely performative uses.

I could not have written this text without having had the opportunity to initiate a line of research that began in 2015 with the study of the early works of Jacques Lacan and culminated in the publication of the book *Lacan, from Wallon to Kojève*.[1] This essay on Lacan's nascent work led me to highlight the decisive step he took in introducing the "mirror stage," which involves the young child's entrance into a relationship with language and with others in the form of an alienation both in the symbolic and in the image of the other. This is so crucial that one can argue that the relationship to one's own body is only possible thanks to language and the relationship to the other.

Thus, before the study of the "mirror stage" can be complete, we must recognize the very early and even necessary incidence of the symbolic world, which constitutes what other currents today refer to as the "prerequisites of language"—not language as such, even in the form of symbols—but rather the very conditions of possibility for access to a world organized by the symbolic. We thus discover that these Lacanian theses are verified today, in the sense that nothing of the subject who lives in the symbolic escapes this fundamental dependence, that which made the poet write, "I is another."

It is therefore starting from research on the beginning of Lacan's work that the study of this Lacanian invention (the object a) imposed itself on me as a theoretical necessity in order to make coherent a conception of the unconscious that leaves little to chance. The more one starts from the early stages of development, the closer one comes to this concept that is both clinical and formal, to the point that it alone constitutes the gravitational point of Freud's discovery. In order to arrive at the clearest possible definition of this new concept, it was then necessary not only to master psychoanalytic conceptual tools but also to take an interest in observations made by other specialists in childhood and experimental psychology. Finally, I believe that in the following pages I demonstrate the theoretical and practical conditions that allowed Lacan to shape the concept of object a, an emergence that is not unrelated to his own nascent work.

Introducing the object a will only be possible if one is equipped with the key concepts established by Lacan: the concept of desire as mediation and therefore as ternary structure, that of the object—which is very different from what psychoanalysis describes with this term—and, not to mention, the original contribution of the mirror stage, which combines the symbolic and the imaginary. It will take, however, yet another step to detect what allowed Lacan to conceptualize this object a: some fundamental clinical observations drawn from his practice with children as well as experimental observations. Both of these allowed Lacan to note this space that exists between being and the other, a space that emerges only in a punctual and evanescent form, which is the definition of the Lacanian subject. In this way, the function "object a" arises from the relationship between the presence and absence of the living and the other, to the extent that if the function object a is, for Lacan, "the object of objects," its principal example would seem to be the gaze. The gaze is therefore what is before and after life, like the images found in caves—the only traces of beings subjected to the symbolic, and which continue to look back at us even today.

Thus, in the following pages, we will begin by providing a negative definition of the object a, starting from the hypothesis that it is because there cannot be a direct relationship with objects of desire that the function object a proves necessary. Then we will develop a positive definition of the object a by following Lacan's very patient work on the register he calls the imaginary, which for some may seem paradoxical, since his famous return to Freud is achieved by questioning and distancing the importance of the imaginary instance, particularly in analytical practice. But I will also develop entire sections of Lacanian teaching through the deployment of what must appear to us as a positivity in his theory, not only therefore a definition by default of the object a in its fluctuating relationship to the desire that constitutes it, but also as modalities of the being of what is called the unconscious. Indeed, if through psychoanalysis the subject turns out to be anything but a "subject," hence what philosophy and psychology believe they can define as the very agent of consciousness, as the autonomy of the human, then it is precisely this subject that must be understood as rather nonautonomous, as passive, and ultimately, as an effect. If psychoanalysis is to be relevant today, then it must be acknowledged that it is the subject that becomes object.

Note

1 Lucchelli J. P., *Lacan, de Wallon à Kojève*, Ed. Michèle, Paris, 2017.

Chapter 1

The Primacy of the Symbolic

The object a is certainly one of the most original concepts in Lacan's work. It is so original that the term "concept" itself may not be entirely adequate when it comes to describing this invention. One might even go so far as to say that the word "object" doesn't quite fit either, which is why the phrase "the object a is a concept" would contain two misleading elements. In this regard, when defining the object a, it is worth remembering that, for Lacan, the notion of the object corresponds only to a metaphorical use of the term "object[1]," which implies that it doesn't correspond to what is referred to by this term in psychoanalysis or in philosophy, or even to what Lacan himself called "object" before the introduction of this new notion. It will therefore be crucial, in a first approach to the object a, to define what Lacan means by "object." In particular, it will be necessary to discern how it is opposed to other uses of the concept of "object" as employed in psychoanalysis.

One might think that Lacan's famous seminar titled *The Four Fundamental Concepts of Psychoanalysis*[2] actually describes five concepts, since it is in this seminar that Lacan formalizes what he calls the object a, an object that had already been introduced in the previous year's seminar, which dealt with anxiety. But it would be a mistake to consider the object a as a concept in itself unless one considers that it functions in relation to the four fundamental concepts in a precise manner. Transference, repetition, the unconscious, and drive: these four concepts are related to the object a, and this is precisely why they are necessarily fundamental concepts, defining both the praxis and the theory of psychoanalysis as conceived by Lacan. I could thus advance this initial hypothesis: the fundamental concept in Lacan is what designates a concept that requires the object a to be defined as such; in other words, it is the set of terms that maintain a close and necessary relationship with the object a but that are not this object. Indeed, transference and repetition as phenomena linked to the analytic cure, and the unconscious and the drive as terms taken from Freud's metapsychology, are all in a relationship of tension with the object a. Understanding psychoanalytic praxis and theory in this manner is inconceivable if we do not prioritize a primary reference to the notion of lack, but what kind of lack are we talking about? In order to avoid making too opaque a use of terms that are widely overused in Lacanian theory, I propose to clarify what one should initially understand by lack.

DOI: 10.4324/9781003614203-1

What Do We Call "Object" in Psychoanalysis?

Since we are going to deal with the object a, it seems evident that we should first take an interest in the definition of the object in psychoanalysis, a definition that is far from univocal and that for this reason deserves our keenest interest and necessitates our greatest rigor. I will therefore, for a few pages, set aside the notion of the object a to focus as closely as possible on what we can call the object in psychoanalysis. To achieve any kind of elaboration of the object in psychoanalysis, to construct a theory of the object, Lacan needed practically the first ten years of his seminar before arriving at the seminar on anxiety, where he deals for the first time with this "non-shareable[3]" object, what he calls the object a. But if this new object a is nonshareable, then any prior definition of the object in psychoanalysis necessarily involves, at this stage of Lacanian elaboration, the notions of sharing, exchange, and symbolic gift. We must start, in my opinion, from this first point of reference: the notion of sharing, as imaginary as it may seem, is crucial in understanding the notion of object in psychoanalysis. One can even keep in mind this initial definition of the object: we call object anything that is of the order of sharing and that cannot not be shared. In this sense, the notion is not only imaginary and must be defined according to the symbolic hypothesis of the gift. Thus, the object, the mediation of the gift (through exchange), and sharing is the markers of what introduces and maintains the speaking being on to the path of language. This language, this exchange (which necessarily implies rules), structures the living being that is subject to it, but we will see that it also involves a certain definition, not only theoretical but also practical, of lack.

The Lack of Object and the Preeminence of the Symbolic

To construct a return to Freud, to reconstruct psychoanalytic theory in such a way that it responds to Freud's inaugural step—namely the discovery of the unconscious as a formal structure, as a language that has a permanent effect on life—Lacan needed an entire year of teaching to introduce his audience to what should be understood by the word "object" in psychoanalytic practice, and this was solely to introduce them to the very Freudian notion of the "lack of object[4]." To put it bluntly, according to Lacan, there is no object in psychoanalysis without an inherent dimension of lack, a lack produced or generated by the very structure of language. Let's be clear: it is not that language is a structure that enslaves the living being but rather that if the living being can only exist through language, then language leaves that being at a certain distance from the world and life, as well as from everything that is of the order of the possible, the desirable, and the representable.

The first question that one must therefore ask is, what does Lacan mean by the phrase "lack of object"? What I mean to formulate with this question is the fact that before Lacan, one never spoke in psychoanalysis of a lack of object. To define this original concept, we must therefore understand what is meant by lack and by object.

By defining each of these terms, we will have a better chance of making the phrase "lack of object" more intelligible. In order to tackle the "object relationship"—a concept he intends to criticize to the point that in the second session of the said seminar, he advises no longer using the phrase "object relationship"—Lacan had to define the object from a psychoanalytic perspective, making abstraction of imaginary categories such as "archaic object" and other entities that aimed to give the object a status closer to the truth.

It is by hypothesizing the preeminence of the symbolic, which denaturalizes the relationship to the object as such, that one can envisage a new way of conceiving of the object: in other words, there exists an arbitrary world made up of rules, of very strict implicit codes that constitute however many obligatory passages, however many conditions of access to the world and to the other. It is therefore understood that there is no object in the traditional, empirical sense of the term. For psychoanalysis, the concrete, pragmatic object has no consistency. In other words, for Lacan, the other—whether real or imaginary, the material objects of desire and/or need, the most dignified or the most ignoble vital sustenance—all of this would be the imaginary object, an object that has no value in itself in the sense that all these imaginary objects are equivalent. One object is not worth more than another with regard to the symbolic definition of the object. And what is this symbolic dimension of the object? It is the symbolic register itself, ordered according to signifiers that outline a history in which all signifiers exist only by way of their functional value (according to Saussure's definition of the signifier, namely that a signifier is only valuable in relation to the negativity, opposition, and difference it has in relation to one or many other signifiers).

Lacan's starting point, his first seminar, *Freud's Papers on Technique*, was primarily aimed at correcting the use that psychoanalytic authors had made of Freudian technique, which was too focused on the register he called "imaginary," interpretations constructed from behavioral parameters, wild interventions, and dynamics that deviated from the royal road of the unconscious. Lacan intended to rectify these practices of his colleagues (one need only think of his critique of a case analyzed by Annie Reich). The only remedy: the discriminating isolation of the signifier, what allows one to avoid a certain theoretical and clinical misguidance. This was also, more than ever, the perspective defended by the seminar of the following year on the ego, where Lacan once again sought to separate the imaginary register—the ego—from the one he calls symbolic, producing this new category he calls the "subject". The theoretical beacon of this second seminar is, as we know, the "Z schema" (or "L schema"), introduced during the session of May 25, 1955, which precisely differentiates the symbolic axis from the imaginary axis. Then, after another year dedicated to psychosis—where he continues to defend a distinction between clinical structures and intensifies the difference between the symbolic and the imaginary (to simplify: neurosis is constructed on the notion of repression, and therefore of the symbolic, and psychosis is built on the notion of foreclosure, thus linked to the symbolic)—Lacan moved on to the seminar dedicated to the object relationship. It is in this context that the notion of the lack of object emerges. This seminar is a significant moment in Lacan's teaching, marking the introduction of this new concept, which will become central in his work.

Thus, during the first ten years of his teaching, Lacan primarily addressed what the object was not, if I may put it that way. In other words, concerning our central theme, he approached the object a by default, without mentioning it as such but by assuming it as a necessary effect of the preeminence of the symbolic. So, what is the symbolic? Beginning with his first seminar, as I have already mentioned, Lacan dealt with the symbolic in order to distinguish, within psychoanalysis, the Freudian discovery (defined by its relationship to the signifier) from the specific avatars of analytic experience and practice. What do we see already in Lacan's first seminar? That even when it comes to highlighting the importance of the symbolic, one of the first things Lacan does is to advance the premise that the symbolic is opposed to something else that he will not yet call "the real" but that already holds the place of the real. To elucidate, it is worth citing this long paragraph from the seminar *Freud's Papers on Technique,* where Lacan formulates the following on the topic of repression:

> This important articulation shows us that originally, for repression to be possible, there must be a beyond of repression, something final, already primitively constituted, an initial nucleus of the repressed, which not only is unacknowledged, but which, for not being formulated, is literally *as if it didn't exist*—I'm just following what Freud says. And nevertheless, in a certain sense, it is somewhere, since, as Freud everywhere tells us, it is the center of attraction, calling up all the subsequent repressions.[5]

And, he goes on to specify, "do hang on to the idea that the primitive nucleus is to be found at another level from that of the derivatives of repression," in other words, on a different level than the symbolic that he is trying to introduce and that is ultimately supposed to define the object. This means that even when articulating the primacy of the symbolic, it is essential, due to this setup, to introduce what escapes the symbolic. This separation is crucial and, according to Lacan, lies at the root of Freud's discovery. The avatars of repression are not the same as the primitive core that Lacan wants to save from the generalized confusion reigning among psychoanalysts. The return of the repressed and repression are one and the same, but only on the condition that we understand that the primordial repressed, the so-called "primitive core," cannot be articulated by the signifier. The signifier can only miss it. In short, the unconscious is not the "id." The primitive core, by "not being formulated" (let us remember the late Lacan and his oft-repeated phrases regarding the repressed, such as "not ceasing to not write itself" or "ceasing to not write itself"),[6] is not symbolizable as such—it resists the symbolic.

With this initial positioning, we find ourselves within a reasoning that clearly distinguishes the unconscious as that which is governed by the laws of signifiers (we have only to reread the *Traumdeutung* or the example of the forgetting of the name Signorelli) from the id insofar as it represents the real and, as Freud says, "the silence of the drives," a phrase that Lacan will take up in his seminar on *The Four Fundamental Concepts of Psychoanalysis*, where he precisely formalizes the object a. I am not rushing to equate the object a with the "core of the repressed," but once again, we see from the outset in Lacanian theory a *Spaltung* ("splitting") between the symbolic register and the repressed as such.

Let us therefore keep in mind this distinction: the unconscious is not the id. Lacan continues the same reading of Freud in his seminar the following year, the seminar on the ego to which I have already referred. In the chapter titled "Introduction to the Entwurf," it is crucial for Lacan to place the study and highlighting of metapsychology at the center of his study of the ego, particularly Freud's 1920 text "Beyond the Pleasure Principle."[7] He thus values the drives—the "silence of the drives"—in order to contrast them with the nonsilence of the signifier in a rather peculiar way, as he reads Freud's *Project* with an interest in cybernetics.

The Signifier and Loss

It was in the early 1950s that Lacan became interested in cybernetics through the work of Claude Lévi-Strauss. The cyberneticists, notably Norbert Wiener,[8] aimed to promote cybernetics in terms of both the theoretical paradigm shift it brought about and its potential practical implications for the human sciences and society in general. They took into account the discoveries of physiologists (notably Walter Cannon and his concepts of homeostasis and feedback),[9] and it was in this context that Lacan indicated, "Among the energy equivalences we can apprehend with respect to a living organism, we can only really know about metabolism, that is, the balance sheet what goes in and what comes out.[10]"

It may seem curious that when Lacan addresses the issue of loss—in this specific case, the loss of energy—he refers to the organism, to biology. But upon closer examination, it is not so surprising since for him, the organism and the biological are nothing other than machines subject to the signifier, a signifier that compels us to think of the notion of loss as the necessary product of a machine. I will show that to introduce the object of anxiety, and the object a along with it, Lacan will discuss the physiological phenomenon of penile detumescence and its effects on the speaking being, reflecting a kind of real of the organism that does not necessarily fit into the pathways of the signifier.

So, let's go back. When it comes to energy equivalences in the organism, we have at our disposal only the ledger—"what comes in and what goes out"—which means precisely this: "but about everything that happens inside, we know absolutely nothing.[11]" Again, Lacan intends to set aside what is not strictly ordered according to the lines of the signifier and the laws that govern it (metaphor, metonymy, various combinations). It is clear that we are again touching upon that domain of the system where, if the unconscious is the place of accounting (what comes in and what goes out)—that is to say, the unconscious and the Freudian discovery conceived of specifically from the point of view of the symbolic (dreams, slips of the tongue, witticisms)—this does not exhaust the entirety of the unconscious.

The id, the core of the repressed, is not to be confused with the symbolic because we know nothing about "what is inside" and, to repeat the expression from the seminar on *Freud's Papers on Technique* already mentioned, "it is literally as if it did not exist." If we want to follow Lacan's approach, we must therefore distinguish from the outset the ledger—the signifier—from the id—the silence of the drives—a silence whose persistence is echoed in the silence of the analyst. Thus, at the beginning of his teaching, in recentering both psychoanalytic theory and practice around the primacy of the symbolic (different from the imaginary but also from the real), Lacan introduces, at the very heart of the symbolic, the id—the drives, loss, and lack—as being essentially what resists symbolization.

What is the importance of this primacy of the symbolic? Put differently, why does it seem decisive for analytic practice? There is a sort of "hyperstructuralism" in Lacan. Let's not shy away from the word—the idea is advanced by Jean-Claude Milner when he discusses Lacan's "first classicism," namely the one that posits the symbolic along with a structural definition of the signifier.[12] In this sense, hyperstructuralism is the acknowledgment of the main axiom of structuralism, namely that the value of a term is determined only by the position it occupies in relation to other terms. This is crucial in the definition of the object in his seminar *The Object Relation*, for it means that the object is not valued for its intrinsic properties but is rather determined by the signifier.

What does this imply for our analytic experience? To give an example, it means that if your patient dreams of an old lady, it is useless to interpret this as "it's his mother" when on the contrary, the old lady is only valuable in relation to a young woman. The same can be said of phobias, where the phobic object itself is of no importance. It could be anything—a spider, a shark—regardless of whether the phobic person lives near the beach. That phobia is a "hub"—like the definition of *mana* conceived as a "floating signifier" according to Lévi-Strauss[13]—clearly indicates that the (imaginary) properties of the object have no value for the unconscious; in this way Freud could stipulate that the unconscious does not know time, contradiction, or even sexual difference.

As already mentioned, one of the main consequences of the primacy of the symbolic is the ternary structure of the signifier, which does not necessarily correspond to Jakobson's structuralist approach. I'll quote Lacan on this subject:

> There first has to be a libidinal element that picks out a particular object qua object. This object becomes a signifier in the subject, occupying the place that will henceforth be called the ego-ideal. Desire, on the other hand, undergoes a substitution—another desire takes its place. This other desire doesn't come from nothing, it's not nothing. It existed before—it related to the third term—and it emerges transformed.[14]

This quotation from Lacan, which evokes the ternary aspect of the subject's relationships to its objects, allows us to understand what will be at stake for the psychoanalyst concerning the Oedipus complex. We know how wary Lacan is of this

Freudian concept: in the 1950s, he treated the Oedipus complex as an imaginary reference, but very quickly he sought to rid himself of the imaginary trap by treating it as a structure, as we perceive it in his quotation. What exactly does this structure determine? An indirect relationship to the world.

Why Is There No Direct Relationship to the World?

How do we connect with others and share with them what we want, feel, know, etc.? Perhaps to find a satisfactory answer, we should look at how infants—and more broadly, babies and young children—interact with others, especially those close to them. It seems that the first type of exchange that a baby (we can even speak of newborns) manages to establish with its mother is primarily through eye-to-eye[15] contact with her. This first type of exchange or connection with the world and with others happens through the visual, giving primacy to vision. This import of vision, entirely biological in the sense that the eyes serve as a powerful means of connection with the world, has been highlighted by psychologists, psychoanalysts, and experimental studies, all of which emphasize that the musculature of the eyes, alongside the muscles of sucking, is the most developed in infants and young babies.[16] There is certainly much to consider regarding these two muscle groups that surround two anatomical "holes" (the mouth and the eyes), as they function like sphincters that allow the infant to both cling to and separate from (to individualize, in a certain sense) others. In both a literal and a figurative sense, these sphincters constitute "borders," even diaphragms, that connect the child with the world.

From the outset, then, as highlighted by experimental studies, vision and its correlate— the eyes of others—are at the forefront of the very early, ultra-early, development of humans. While the mouth seems at first to be a vital instrument for the infant, the same cannot be said of vision, which as I will show in more depth has a very different regulatory function in the sense that it forms the basis for communication with others and the possibility of sharing. (In a humorous way, one could add that the mouth is also used for communication, but in a manner far more secondary than that of vision, as I plan to explain later.)

As everyone knows, Lacan drew attention, within the psychoanalytic world, to the importance of the eyes and even to the perception of the face in infants and young babies in his text on the "mirror stage.[17]" It is interesting to note that while Freud wrote the *Three Essays on the Theory of Sexuality* to explain the importance of infantile sexuality in the formation of the personality, Lacan makes the gaze—the eye—a more prevalent drive-related border than the drive-related borders of the anal and oral stages. One could even say that this essay will revolve around this observation: when it comes to the construction of the individual, it is much more the other—in what they bring from the symbolic world, from sharing and communication—that prevails rather than an abstract entity that was already there, namely the drive (*Trieb*) that one would more or less successfully domesticate.

Let us therefore address the primacy of the eyes, in other words, the primacy of vision (of the baby) and the gaze of the other (the eyes of the other), which establishes this famous eye-to-eye contact. Several authors (Mundy[18], Rochat[19], Scaife[20], to name a few) see in this first model of exchange with the outside world the definitive beginning and common foundation of communication, speech, and the relationship with the world and others. And this for a very specific reason: this very strong but not necessarily vital connection (less vital than food, let's say) with others quickly becomes not an end in itself but, on the contrary, as we will see, the means through which the baby establishes a relationship with others through a point of support in the other. I emphasize this point: if, at first, the eye-to-eye contact happens very early on, it becomes only the means by which the child can have a relationship with something other than the person with whom they establish this contact. It is as if this mode of relationship were not bidirectional but rather "tridirectional," as if it sealed our relationship to the world through another, through a thirdness or a ternary structure, and this far beyond an improbable "subject–object" relationship (the famous "object" from which we started and toward which we will maintain the utmost suspicion).

Lacan, for his part, formulated the idea that it is through the image of the other ("mirror stage") that the young child, between six and eighteen months, manages to have an imaginary notion of their own body. In this sense, the image of the other (whether the image of another young child or that of an adult) serves as a kind of prosthesis for the human being. In this way, even if they do not have the physical strength to assume, in the proprioceptive sense, the notion of "[my] own body," they can still imagine that they have it through the complete image of the other's body. I have demonstrated elsewhere[21] how much this thesis owes to Henri Wallon and how it differs from it. What I am interested in demonstrating here is not limited to one's own body, but goes far beyond it, in the sense that the visual relationship with the other (and its practical means: the gaze of the other) will allow the child to incorporate language and, through this means, to apprehend one's own body as one of the elements of language.

Thus, long before the perception of one's own body as such and the possibility of spoken language, the individual can rely on the other to grasp, understand, and represent the world, its objects, and its peers. The infant relies on the other or, more precisely, on something in the other, namely their eyes. It may seem surprising that the child relies on this part of the body to access the symbolic, given that it is precisely that part of the other's body that is the most unpredictable and the least constant, the least subject to regularities. It is also the part in the other that most conveys intentions, desires, and communication. A gaze carries an intention no matter what it is, which makes the other much more than a thing or an object. And this is all the more true because it will precisely serve the baby to enter social cognition, to go beyond the face-to-face or the eye-to-eye. A relationship with others and with the world can only be established through the intervention of another human being, a bearer of intention and desires. In this sense, the gaze of the other, this particular part of their face, is the most human thing because it is also the other's most elusive part.

Even before there is a symbolization of the world, we have this point of anchorage in the other that is a point of reference for the infant as well in the sense that they too are an "object" of the other's gaze (at least we can hypothesize this), an observable object that carries carrying intentions, desires, etc. It is interesting to remember that very early on, under the influence of the philosopher Alexandre Kojève, Lacan hypothesized that desire in humans is desire primarily determined by the desire of the other. This means that in one way or another, human desire is conditioned and alienated by the desire of the other. There is no other desire than that which is mediated by the intervention of the other as being at the basis of access to the symbolized world, a symbol that is therefore conditioned because it is also a symbol for the other. The individual anticipates or is "anticipated" by the symbolic that is already there in the sense that it forms a certain type of functioning configuration, a kind of living syntax.

To give an example, on one occasion I was facing a four-and-a-half-month-old baby and, wanting to touch his little hand, I reached out my hand toward his; he then shifted his gaze to a bottle that was very close to him, almost between him and me. The window in front of him, which is the screen of possibilities ready to be invested by his gaze and mine, by our hints of shared interest or intentions, constrains us to certain movements: my hand, my gaze, his response through his own gaze. One could say that my gaze "becomes" an intention in me, in this case, the intention to grab a bottle, even though my real intention was to stroke the baby's little hand.

Neither for the subject nor for the other do things happen as expected; very early on, there is no true relationship between the two, and on the contrary, a sort of misunderstanding prevails. If we stick to this very simple example—simple in the literal sense of the word, meaning that it cannot be made any simpler, more basic, or more minimal—we observe: 1) the fact that the baby assigns an intention to the other because he has shifted his gaze to an object; 2) the fact that he mistakes the object (the bottle instead of the hand) because he anticipates my gesture, which is an essential point; 3) the fact that in mistaking the object, he does not see, he did not see, that the object of the intention was a part of his own body, that is to say, he does not see, in the screen that is offered to him, his own body on this screen; he is blind to his own body—he scotomizes it.

At first, one might consider that these points are like two sides of the same coin. Attributing an intention or desire to the other involves both the choice of an object (of the Other's desire) and the bracketing of the true object one is aiming at because it is more like a "bet" (a bet on an intention in the other, whom we do not exactly know). The key probably lies in the detection of an intention in the other. I have also just said that there is primarily an anticipation, an anticipation that goes hand in hand with a spatial configuration; anticipation concerns time, but time only makes sense within the spatiality offered to the individual.

In a sense, one could say that it is "human" to detect an intention, a desire, or a life in the other by attributing to it a sign, that is, by finding some sort of explanation for it. It is especially human to find meaning in it, to annihilate it with a response (the meaning generated by anticipation) that will silence what truly arises as intention or desire. If we start from the idea that the gaze of the other implies life and the unpredictable, the anticipation with which the baby participates in it is already a response that attempts to place that living gaze, to find a form for what has no form (the nascent desire in the other). Why is the baby's anticipation an anticipation? Why is it synchronized with the other but poorly synchronized?

A first element of the answer would suppose that the baby's anticipatory gesture tries to make what is unpredictable in the other predictable. Since our intention is to address the object a as a function, we can provisionally name the object a function as this gap between anticipation and the effects it produces, between the unpredictability of life manifesting in the other and the need for predictability (also essential for life). The goal of symbolization, by which I mean the primacy of the symbolic register, is to make "familiar" what is unfamiliar.

There is thus a sort of misunderstanding, where the real referent (this or that object in reality) becomes secondary in relation to the need for familiarity, for predictability, that the living being needs in order to be in the world, to live in it with others. On the one hand, the available visual field serves as a screen (even in the sense of a computer or television screen) and hides the "true" object targeted by the desire of the other, but it hides it by granting it an intention. Thus, the object mistakenly chosen by the baby (the bottle) is not as insignificant as we might think: it is a visible object within the screen constituted by his visual field, a field that is reduced in two ways (having been reduced as a visual field and being composed of only a few discernible elements). On the other hand, and inexorably, many objects remain outside the screen, the majority even, as the choice to be made among the available objects is limited. This hidden part, which does not appear in the visual field, also (and perhaps above all?) concerns the baby's own body (his hand, in this case).

Shared Life

We must go further still. Observations made both in clinical settings and in laboratories with young children lead us to consider what is called joint or shared attention and to understand what can be called, with Simon Baron-Cohen, the shared attention mechanism in the sense that shared attention is simply attention and human socialization. What is joint attention? It is the ability to share an interest in an object or situation with another person.[22] Joint attention is linked to vision (even if it is not the only sense involved) and is by far the primary perception involved in the socialization of babies. As I have already indicated, shared attention occurs in at least two stages: 1) the exchange of gazes (in fact, it is about the vision of the other's eyes, eye to eye) during the first months of life (this phenomenon occurs very early on and would exist from the first days of life) and 2) the fact that between four and six months, the baby's gaze begins to "follow" both the gaze of the other and especially the direction of the other's gaze, independently of the object being looked at (what is "primary" is the fact of following the other's eyes as such—which becomes almost an "endless means"). Thanks to this latter point, there is anticipation, since the child is captivated by the other's gaze and the attention is captured, caught (in Lacan's words). Let's push our reasoning even further. As mentioned, in social communication, which exists long before the existence of speech, humans mistake the (real) referent and, even more so, can only be mistaken since the only true referent is nothing other than the gaze of the other as such. In a certain way, since the baby's vision only follows that of the adult, that vision is, in some sense, their own, or the baby's own vision (the adult "looks," sees in their place). If the child scotomizes their own body, it is because, as it is, their subjective spatiality does not need it; the other's body suffices. Why not suppose that following the gaze of the other is already nothing more than imitating them? One's own body is therefore secondary; what is primary is the gaze of the other that "signifies," through an intention (a desire), the world.

But let us not rush to understand too quickly, and let us be wary of the term "intention." Indeed, the eye itself has a particularity, which is that it can see everything but cannot see itself (just as one does not hear their own voice when speaking); this observation certainly has a heuristic purpose, but it is also relevant because it helps us understand that a human being (just like an animal, for that matter) is never truly objectified by themselves. They can only be objectified from the perspective of another—let us be clear: from the perspective of the Other. I quote Philippe Rochat, who writes:

> The perception of others as intentional entities opens up a new horizon of development in the child. This horizon is an evaluative horizon of the self in relation to others. The other, for the child, becomes a mirror of the self or a social mirror as Lacan and Merleau-Ponty have discussed. At 14 months, we have shown that the child is ostentatiously and explicitly sensitive when someone imitates their own actions. . . . Clearly, they begin to recognize themselves, in other words, to identify with the other.[23]

If, as mentioned, there is no direct relationship with the world, then one's own body, as part of the world, does not offer any privileged access either; the fact that in the child, and from the beginning, there is a distinction between interoceptive, proprioceptive, and exteroceptive spheres[24] clearly shows that one's own body is an assemblage, just like any other object. One might even suppose that in some respects it is the exteroceptive sphere that takes precedence, as indicated by Rochat in the citation above, but also by Lacan in his 1938 text *Les complexes familiaux* (*Family Complexes*).

The Ternary Structure

I mentioned earlier what cognitive psychology calls the "prerequisites of speech." These constitute a set of cues that allow the child to speak almost automatically given their social environment, incorporating, for example, their native language. The incorporation of language occurs intuitively, almost by imitation: one learns the names of things as well as how to construct sentences, to encode and decode, both in the receptive and expressive senses of language—that is, in the sense of understanding as well as of expression—long before anyone explains it to them. The fact that language is primarily social, coming from interactions with others, is illustrated by the fact that, for example, one learns to speak well before learning to read. The signifier, in the linguistic sense, is primarily a sound material, not a visual material (the reading of characters, for example). A table is a table because it is named such and because it is used as a "table"; both the naming of the object and its "functionality" come to us from our relationship with others. The negative proof of this language function is seen in autism, where the table in question: 1) is not a total object in the sense of functionality (the autistic child may spend time stroking the smooth surface of the table, which beyond being a self-sensory experience indicates that the object does not function as a set of relations, that it is not attributed a functionality); 2) does not have a "sound" name: it is through echolalic learning or by reading that the child may name the object "table." In the case of autism, social knowledge will not be intuitive (and therefore it will not be "social").

Cognitive sciences have developed what is known as the theory of mind. I do not intend to elaborate on this at length and refer readers to my book on autism where I explain the theory of mind in more detail.[25] What matters for us here is that we consider how an author like Baron-Cohen explains the prerequisites of speech. To put it briefly, one could say that the infant first has a tendency to detect the gaze of others, or anything in the other that resembles eyes, and then (at six to nine months, though this chronology varies by author), the baby will have a tendency to look at what the other is observing. These are the different components of what the author calls the shared-attention mechanism.

According to Baron-Cohen,[26] who interprets autism based on a deficit in theory of mind and simultaneously highlights the presence of a "social brain" in humans,[27] there are four components in the functioning of a "mindreading" system, components that exhibit increasing complexity: 1) the intentionality detector, 2) the gaze direction detector, 3) shared attention, 4) the theory of mind. For Baron-Cohen, and thanks to the theory of a social brain, which is at the base of the theory of mind—according to which we live in relation to others because we guess their intentions or desires long before we really know what the other wants or intends to do (for example, through what is called empathy)—it is obvious that there is no other relationship to things and others except through the theory of mind, thus through the other. The schema conceived by Baron-Cohen is therefore tripartite: at the base, there are the prerequisites of speech (long before the child can speak); we only have the gaze of the other and their relationship to the world (objects, situations, people), including the act of naming this world. In this schema, we have the adult's gaze (their eyes and the intention and movements of the eyes), the child's vision, and the entire world represented as three distinct elements within a square (Figure 1.1).

Regarding gaze direction, Baron-Cohen specifies that while the intention detector involves different senses (hearing, vision, touch), the gaze direction detector involves only vision. The author draws his readers' attention to the fact that this mechanism involves three functions: 1) it detects the presence of eyes or anything that resembles eyes; 2) it detects whether the eyes are directed at the observer or elsewhere; and 3) it implies that if an organism is looking at something, then it sees that something. This last function is important because it allows the child to attribute a perceptual state to another organism. If the intention detector detects a will, the gaze direction detector will detect what the agent sees. Baron-Cohen emphasizes what has long been known (Lacan): that infants tend to look at their mother's eyes more than at any other part of her face.[28]

The other crucial function related to this tendency in infants is detecting the direction of the eyes within a face. Let's pass over the fact that Baron-Cohen infers that if the other is looking at something, the infant is looking at that same thing; we don't quite see how the infant could engage in such introspection (it is rather the result of imitation, first and foremost, and then, in a second phase, it could become a sort of observation). This assumption nonetheless has the merit of emphasizing the desire or intentionality of others. This corresponds to what authors call "primary intersubjectivity," which then allows for establishing secondary intersubjectivity involving a third party:

> Intersubjective skills enable the construction of singular thought. These skills evolve as vision matures, aided by motor development such as postural control and object manipulation from 3–4 months on. . . . From primary

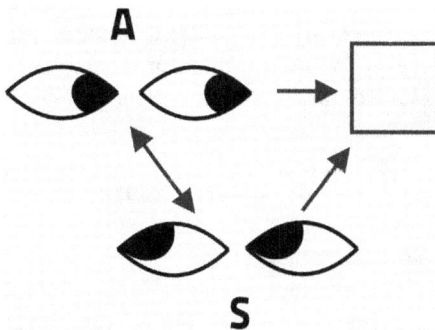

Figure 1.1 The shared attention mechanism.

Source: Baron-Cohen, S., *Mindblindness: An essay on autism and theory of mind*, Boston, The MIT Press, 1995.

intersubjectivity, which is a dual relationship, the baby evolves towards secondary intersubjectivity, which integrates a triadic or cooperative relationship: the child integrates and coordinates their attention with another person and an object; or with two other people. In this developmental dynamic, it is around 9 months that we clearly observe secondary intersubjectivity in which joint attention develops.[29]

The Lacanian Model: The Optical Experiment of the "Inverted Bouquet"

I will not delve into the technical details of the optical experiment introduced by Lacan in 1954 during his first seminar at the Sainte-Anne Hospital, known as the "inverted bouquet experiment." It was in 1936 and later in 1949 that Lacan introduced an initial formulation related to optics under the name "mirror stage," which I will discuss further later. It was indeed in a text titled "The Mirror Stage as Formative of the *I* Function as Revealed in Psychoanalytic Experience" (better known as "The Mirror Stage") that Lacan formulated his first reflections developed from a psychoanalytic perspective. This text is a reworking of a text presented in 1949 in Zurich that itself was based on the main points of another one of Lacan's presentations, partially presented to the public in Marienbad in 1936.

For methodological reasons, one should start from the first published occurrence of the mirror stage, namely the one found in *Les complexes familiaux*. Regarding the mirror stage hypothesis, I demonstrated in another work (though I am aware that others preceded me) that there is a strong likelihood that it originates from the texts of Henri Wallon collected in *Les origines du caractère chez l'enfant* (*The Origins of Character in the Child*), the first of which were written in 1931.[30]

What is the hypothesis of the mirror stage? That there is a motor and neurological insufficiency at birth in humans and that this insufficiency is somewhat compensated for by the vision of one's peers, such as the mother. The infant is psychologically and biologically "fragmented," Lacan asserts. The image of the other thus gives the infant the sensation of organic and psychological unity. Lacan's hypothesis is called the mirror stage because it describes the behavior of the young child in front of the mirror, particularly between the ages of six and eighteen months.

Even as a small child, the baby becomes agitated in front of the mirror and remains captivated by their own image, which suggests that they are also captivated by the image of others and by their surroundings, which also function as mirrors. These clinical descriptions were already noted by various observers (Darwin, Preyer, Guillaume), and Henri Wallon summarized in his book. But that is not all: there is another fundamental clinical element (also described by Wallon, who draws from other observers) that is an integral part of the normal development of the child. The child's behavior in front of the mirror is not complete, not fulfilled, and, to put it bluntly, not normal, if it is not accompanied by a sort of "gesture" (Wallon's word). Darwin was the first to describe this gesture while observing his son:

> When four and a half months old, he repeatedly smiled at my image and his own in a mirror, and no doubt mistook them for real objects; but he showed sense in being evidently surprised at my voice coming from behind him. Like all infants he much enjoyed thus looking at himself, and in less than two months perfectly understood that it was an image; for if I made quite silently any odd grimace, he would suddenly turn round to look at me.[31]

Wallon places great importance on this turning gesture, arguing that the child thereby realizes that there is simultaneity between real objects and virtual objects. However, Lacan does not mention this "turning" in his text on the mirror stage, and it will take until the 1960s for him to talk about it, attributing a crucial role to it in psychic functioning and in the symbolization of the ego, precisely.

In 1938, he is content to describe the child's waste of energy as he jubilates in front of his own image. It will take until the 1950s for him to mention in his psychoanalysis seminar the optical schema of the inverted bouquet, which he describes as a "substitute for the mirror stage." In other words, the inverted bouquet schema is a kind of complement that was missing from the mirror stage for a very simple reason: it introduces the gaze of the other in the form of an eye that "guarantees" and confirms the child's vision of himself in the mirror, namely his own body.

But what in fact was missing from the mirror stage? It was missing not only the eye of the other but above all what it implies, namely the child's turning gesture toward the adult, which Wallon already describes in 1931 and revisits in 1934 in his book *Les origines du caractère chez l'enfant*. So, what is the so-called inverted bouquet experiment? It shows how, thanks to a concave mirror and depending on the angle from which one looks, one can see the images of two different objects combined into a single image that is then reflected on a flat mirror. All it takes is for one to "move," to change the angle or point of view, for the unified image to break apart. But the key lies in the fact that the child's eye needs the presence of another "eye" to validate the reality of what is seen (Figure 1.2).[32]

The symbol $ indicates the subject facing an image (their own and/or those of other objects in the world). They see things on a flat "mirror," that is, where objects and people are visible in everyday reality. These are visible and, most importantly, comprehensible, according to the gaze that the subject ($) shares with another, making them assimilable in the game of desire, in the socialized world. This "other" with whom $ shares and exchanges glances is, in the schema, represented by a concave mirror, which allows for the socialized perception of objects (things, situations, people, intentions, desires, metaphors, etc.).

By following this experiment, Lacan complicates his initial schema of the mirror stage, adding another mirror to show more forcefully the necessity of maintaining a "point of view," a certain position of the eye or another structure that is meant to be "fixed," so that the image perceived is unified and complete (it involves

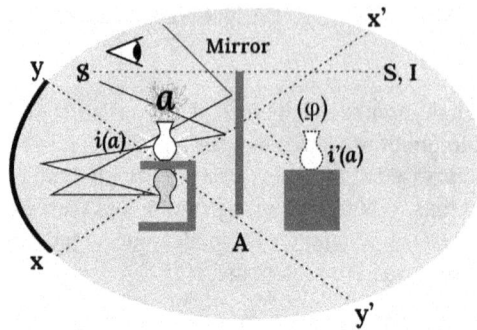

Figure 1.2 The inverted bouquet optical schema.

seeing separate real images in a single reflected image: a bouquet of flowers, on one side, and a vase that will serve as its container in the total image on the other). I will quote Lacan, who clarifies things regarding his optical model:

> For the Other where discourse is situated, which is always latent in the triangulation that consecrates this distance, is not latent as long as it extends all the way to the purest moment of the specular relation: to the gesture by which the child at the mirror turns toward the person who is carrying him and appeals with a look to this witness; the latter decants the child's recognition of the image, by verifying it, from the jubilant assumption in which it certainly *already was*.[33]

Thus, the crucial element in the optical schema is found in the introduction of a point of view that allows the concave mirror to produce the impression of a total image, which Lacan calls "the Other" and which adds to the perception one has in front of the flat mirror, that is, a child's own image (and/or those of the world) that gives the child a psychological unity. This artifice is therefore necessary to justify the fact that the young child "turns" toward the one who witnesses the perception of the child's body image reflected in the mirror, as well as the relevance, existence, and functionality of other objects. Let us clarify further this important remark about this third instance, which might lead us to imagine that it corresponds to the place of the father: it does not. Lacan pertinently points out, "But this already should not mislead us about the structure of the presence that is here evoked as a third: it owes nothing to the anecdote of the character who embodies it."

Lacan thus gives a status to the body such that it is compatible with the ego, so compatible that they merge into one. The body and the ego are therefore continuous without interruption. This is quite a significant assertion because why would the image of the body, to take just this aspect of the imaginary, be so important? Can a being only reflect itself as an image in order to have a perception of itself? This image of the being, "as it sees itself," places it, on the one hand, outside of itself, as it sees itself as if it, the being, were an other.

On the other hand, this image is its most present being, the most radical version of itself (or at least it claims to be). In a sense, this image that I see reflected is already the other: why? For a very simple reason, which is that it is perceived from the perspective of this other. The body as such is already the effect of the "killing of the thing,[34]" as is any object in the socialized world. As everyone knows, even if Lacan evokes the word "murder," it is a murder that gives life and desire. Murder here is not synonymous with "death," quite the opposite. Here is an example: if we call "social cognition" the effect of the symbolic, that is, the act of annihilating an empirical "object" as such to grant it a function, it is precisely because the object as such is not necessary in itself. If a child can play with a remote control by making the sound of a small car, it is because the small car itself is no longer necessary, reflecting the killing of the thing. This murder is one that makes the child want to play with the small car; the less accessible the small car is to the child, the "more" they can and want to play with the small car—in this more a notion dear to Lacan appears that I will explore later, namely the *plus-de-jouir* ("surplus enjoyment").

If we want to understand Lacan's schema beyond the status of the body, since it goes without saying that Lacan's optical schema serves to understand our relationship to the symbolic, we could take the example of the small car and the remote control: in place of the real vase in the image (the one on the left), we can place the real "small car," and in place of the reconstituted bouquet (on the right)—reconstituted because, as everyone knows, it is not "really" whole—we can place the remote control. The remote works all the better as a small car because it is nothing other than the perfect product of a social interaction, a murder of the thing, and not a real unsocialized, unnamed small car, like the one the autistic child encounters and with which they do not "know" how to play.[35]

Why is the example of the remote control important? Because it shows that what is decisive is the signifier (the sound of the car's engine made by the child) and not the object as such. Why, then, would psychoanalytic theory be correct in separating the "emptying" of the object (which Lacan writes as $-\varphi$ or even "murder of the thing") and the narcissistic image (either the body or the objects of desire, which Lacan writes as "i(a)")? Because this is how things happen in the humanized world, where one must distinguish the $-\varphi$ of the signifier (for example, the sound of the small car's engine feigned by the child)—which is already a murder of the thing (absence of the real small car)—from the i(a), the object we deal with (in reality, the remote control) which is precisely put aside as such, an object that initially served other purposes.

Convergences and Divergences

It does not take exceptional insight to realize that Lacan's optical schema and Baron-Cohen's schema coincide on practically all points. Put simply, in both cases, we have the young child who can only incorporate themselves into the symbolic and social world through vision (or perception). For both, it is fundamentally through a shared gaze, a gaze from another that provides validation, that creates the world and that can name it as such (traditionally, the adult) that this is realized. In both cases, it is a ternary structure, in which something exists only because it exists for another. The theoretical and descriptive coincidence here is astonishing.

There is however a tangible difference that perhaps summarizes the theoretical and clinical difference between psychoanalysis and cognitive science. In Baron-Cohen's schema, the world and everything that is a symbol, word, thing, or person, is represented by a square (which upon closer inspection is a kind of window that opens onto the world). In Lacan's optical schema, this square is represented by a mirror (a flat mirror, like those we encounter in everyday life) in which is reflected above all the body of the individual, as Lacan names it, with their ego, their "I." It goes without saying that we can add any other image along with that of the person: a bouquet of flowers, a car, the mother, the brothers, in short, the world as we see it, that is, the socialized world, which is anything but "the world as it is" (otherwise, ask the autistic child for whom a "table" is not exactly a table, but a smooth surface, etc.).

In other words, just as Lacan "forgot" to add the gesture of turning toward the adult in his first description of the mirror stage—that is, the gesture of joint attention (even though it was perfectly readable in the pages of Wallon that he surely read)—Baron-Cohen, in turn, forgot to specify that in the square window of his schema, there is also the child's own body, which, in some respects, is just another object in this socialized world. Of course, it is a body that is also socialized, not just a smooth, shiny surface but a body with a surface a little more complex than the table mentioned earlier (a table that is also not just a smooth surface; otherwise, we would all be autistic. It is a table with functionality, a socialized table that will be used to eat snacks, draw, etc.). But Baron-Cohen forgot the body, reducing the world to a simple matter of information (social information, but still, simple information).

To put it succinctly, one could say that with the mirror stage without joint attention—the key to the social—Lacan had conceived a "self-image"; without Wallon's turning gesture, he nearly made everyone autistic, making faces in front of a mirror without knowing what its image is for. And one could also say that Baron-Cohen's schema, a schema that allows us to perceive the world as if we were a computer without a body, nearly turned humans into "transhumans," or minds without bodies—brains in a vat.[36] Thus, Lacan had to construct a more complete and more finished schema that would account for what happens in the living being. This is what, in a certain sense, the optical schema presented in the *Écrits* accomplishes.

It must be acknowledged that in moving from primary to secondary intersubjectivity, the child makes a qualitative leap, a kind of mutation; they are no longer the same. They "repress," in a way, what comes from the other, this first other (the mother or whoever it may be). They precisely repress the "gaze" of the other, a gaze that, as such, the child will no longer see, diverting their vision to other objects in the world (Lacan's flat mirror or Baron-Cohen's square window; see Figure 1.3).

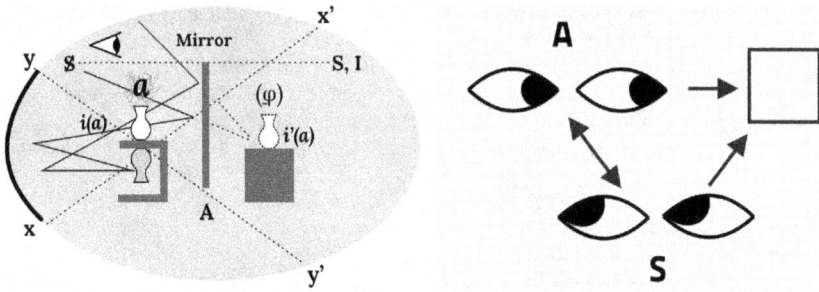

Figure 1.3 Lacan's (1960) (left) and Baron-Cohen's (1992) (right) schemas.

It goes without saying that the gaze of the other as such will never be "seen" in the backdrop of the perceptible and socialized world because even the gaze of the other will be signified, or socialized, just like the remote control. It is precisely by restoring something of the ideal image of the object (the "real" small car from the previous example, the real object from which we are separated, or even the very gaze of the other) to the reflected image in the socialized and functioning world that we can be confronted with a disconcerting reality. Another reality that reminds us that we are in a fictional world, a world that can quickly tip into the uncanny (Freud) or what steps outside of our usual frame. This will be the moment of anxiety, which I intend to explore in the next chapter.

One can easily observe that the two schemas essentially represent the same structure, namely a triangular relationship characterized by mediation, where access to the symbolic world is sustained only by the gaze, the assent, or the participation of another subject. It is in this way that the Lacanian model anticipates by a few decades the research in cognitive sciences around social cognition and the theory of mind, fields that only partially cover the underlying imaginary matrix of the mirror stage.

Notes

1 Lacan J., *Anxiety: The Seminar of Jacques Lacan, Book X*, Polity Press, Malden, 2014, p. 86.
2 Lacan J., *The Four Fundamental Concepts of Psycho-Analysis*, Routledge, 2004.
3 Lacan J., *Anxiety: The Seminar of Jacques Lacan, Book X*, Polity Press, Malden, 2014, p. 91.
4 "These critical remarks bear above all on use of the term *frustration.* This use is in a certain sense legitimised by the fact that what is essential in this dialectic is much rather the lack of object than the object itself", Lacan J., *The Object Relation, The Seminar of Jacques Lacan, Book IV*, translated by A.R. Price, Polity, 2020.
5 Lacan J., *The Seminar of Jacques Lacan, Book 1: Freud's Papers on Technique 1953–1954*, W. W. Norton & Company, 1988, p. 43.
6 "The necessary—what I propose to accentuate for you with this mode—is that which doesn't stop *(ne cesse pas)* what?—being written *(de s'écrire)*", Lacan J., *On Feminine*

Sexuality the Limits of Love and Knowledge: The Seminar of Jacques Lacan, Book XX, Encore, New York, 1998, p. 59.

7 Freud S., "Beyond the pleasure principle", in *The Revised Standard Edition of the Complete Psychological Works of Sigmund Freud*, Volume XVIII, translated by James Strachey and Mark Solms, Rowman & Littlefield, London, 2024.

8 Wiener N., *Cybernetics or Control and Communication in the Animal and the Machine*, M.I.T. Press, Cambridge, MA, 1985.

9 Cannon W., *The Wisdom of the Body*, W. W. Norton & Company, NY, 1963.

10 Lacan J., *The Ego in Freud's Theory and in the Technique of Psychoanalysis, 1954–1955, Book II*, W.W. Norton & Co, 1991, p. 95.

11 Lacan J., *The Ego in Freud's Theory and in the Technique of Psychoanalysis, 1954–1955, Book II*, W.W. Norton & Co, 1991, p. 96.

12 Milner J.-C., *Le périple structural*, Seuil, Paris, 1998.

13 Levi-Strauss C., *Introduction to the Work of Marcel Mauss*, Routdledge, London, 2013.

14 Lacan J., *Formations of the Unconscious: The Seminar of Jacques Lacan*, Polity Press, 2020, p. 279.

15 Rochat P., "The gaze of others", in M. R. Banaji and S. A. Gelman (Eds.), *Navigating the Social World: What Infants, Children, and Other Species Can Teach Us. Oxford Series in Social Cognition and Social Neuroscience*, Oxford University Press, New York, US, 2013, p. 205–211.

16 Johnson S. P. and Johnson K. L., "Early perception-action coupling: Eye movements and the development of object perception", *Infant Behavior and Development, 23*, 2000, p. 461–483.

17 Lacan J., "The mirror stage as formative of the I function", in *Ecrits*, W. W. Norton & Company, 2006.

18 Mundy P. and Newell L., "Attention, joint attention, and social cognition", *Current Directions in Psychological Science, 16*, 2007.

19 Rochat P., "Five levels of self-awareness as they unfold early in life", *Consciousness and Cognition, 12*(4), 2003, p. 717–731.

20 Scaife M. and Bruner J., "The capacity of joint visual attention in the infant", *Nature, 253*, 1975, p. 265–266.

21 Lucchelli J. P., *Lacan, de Wallon à Kojève*, Ed. Michèle, Paris, 2017.

22 Aubineau L.-H., Vandromme L. and Le Driant B., "L'attention conjointe, quarante ans d'évaluations et de recherches de modélisations", *L'Année psychologique, 115*(1), 2015, p. 141–174.

23 Rochat P., "Sens de soi et sens de l'Autre au début de la vie", in A. Berthoz and B. Andrieu (Dir.), *Le corps en acte, Centenaire de Merleau-Ponty*, PUN, Nancy, 2011, p. 64.

24 Wallon H., *Les Origines du caractère chez l'enfant*, PUF, Paris, 1934.

25 Lucchelli J. P., *Autisme, quelle place pour la psychanalyse?* Ed. Michèle, Paris, 2018.

26 Baron-Cohen S., *Mindblindness: An Essay on Autism and Theory of Mind*. The MIT Press, Boston, 1995.

27 Brothers L., "The neural basis of primate social communication", *Motivation and Emotion, 14*(2), 1990, p. 81–91.

28 Maurer D. and Barrera M., "Infants' perception of natural and distorted arrangements of a schematic face", *Child Development, 52*(1), 1981, p. 196–202.

29 Aubineau L.-H., Vandromme L. and Le Driant B., "L'attention conjointe, quarante ans d'évaluations et de recherches de modélisations", *L'Année psychologique, 115*(1), 2015, p. 141–174.

30 Lucchelli J. P., *Lacan, de Wallon à Kojève*, éd. Michèle, Paris, 2018.

31 Darwin C., "A biographical sketch of an infant", *Mind, 2*(7), 1 July 1877, p. 289–290.

32 Lacan J., "Remarks on Daniel Lagache's presentation", in *Ecrits*, W. W. Norton & Company, 2006, p. 565.

33 Lacan J., "Remarks on Daniel Lagache's presentation", in *Ecrits*, W. W. Norton & Company, 2006, p. 568.
34 Lacan J., "The function and field of speech and language in psychoanalysis", in *Ecrits*, W. W. Norton & Company, 2006, p. 262.
35 Interestingly, Lacan constructs his optical schema in relation to the "Dick" case, namely a case of autism.
36 Putnam H., *Reason, Truth and History*, Cambridge University Press, Cambridge, 1982.

Chapter 2

How the Object a Is Deduced from the Imaginary Relationship

In this chapter, I will continue my reconstruction of the theory of the object in Lacan. More specifically, I will situate the status of what he calls object a starting from the imaginary object. Indeed, it may seem paradoxical that after introducing the reader to the status of the Lacanian object based on symbolic coordinates—since Lacan made a significant effort to empty the object, particularly of its imaginary substance—I would now return to the imaginary register that I deliberately set aside in the first chapter in order to grasp another status of this object that interests us: the object a.

In his teaching, Lacan used the term "object petit a" to describe both the imaginary object and this other status of the object, a very different status that will only later give rise to the object a. For there is indeed a reason that pushes us to put the imaginary object and object a into relation: it lies in the very instability of the imaginary register, an instability that reveals the flaws in the symbolic and that can only be detected through various experiences of the living being's failure in the world and with others. If the imaginary register is unstable, it is because the symbolic as such is not without flaws and can only be partially patched up by the imaginary (symptom, fantasy, objects of desire, but also "self-help manuals" and other attempts at mastering the living being) When I say "symbolic" here, I obviously mean what was dealt with in the previous chapter, which can be summarized with the central idea that "the symbol first manifests itself as the killing of the thing.[1]" If it is through the flaws of the symbolic that Freud discovered the unconscious (*Witz*, slips of the tongue, etc.), it is also through the flaws of the imaginary that Freud was able to give a status to castration, in the form, for example, of the uncanny—the correlate to anxiety.

In order to concisely grasp the relationship between the concept I am attempting to define and the imaginary register, we can use the opposition that Lacan establishes between reality and the "real," an opposition that accounts for the distance between the world to which the ego adjusts itself with varying success (reality) and the living being driven by the drive (the real). If reality can be defined as a continuous, coherent whole compatible with the ego, the real in Lacan's terms refers to the discontinuous, incoherent part of the psyche, with its contradictory

DOI: 10.4324/9781003614203-2

and disharmonious aspects in relation to the ego. The deduction of the object a from the imaginary—the ego—and reality must necessarily take into account this incongruous real, which is by definition unsuited to the register of the ego and its narcissistic and imaginary objects. To put it another way: the function of the imaginary is to supplement the division, or the *Spaltung*, inherent in the functioning of the symbolic.[2]

This is why I chose to first establish the primacy of the symbolic—that is, the unconscious structured by the symbolic with the gap it entails—before then situating the imaginary functioning that claims to supplement the gaps inherent in the existence of the unconscious. And what is the unconscious here? It is nothing less than the result of a process related to repression, to the derealization of the world as I described it in the previous chapter, that one plays with a remote control as if it were a toy car (incidentally, the "other scene" as Freud conceived it, following Fechner, is not far removed from this car/remote control dialectic). Let us further clarify: why would the symbolic have these "gaps" (demonstrated by the existence of the unconscious and its formations: *Witz*, slips of the tongue, dreams)? Because the symbolic covers the world by making it arbitrary (a house is a house, a husband is a husband, etc.)—and this is why de Saussure will say that the sign is arbitrary, and why Lacan will call the primacy of the symbolic register the "discourse of the master."

If we start again from the "optical schema" (Lacan/Baron-Cohen), we must admit that there are two points that are "repressed" as such. One concern, as I have said, is that the gaze of the other that leads us to symbolize the world (we can also say "unrealize" it, in the sense that it makes it something other than what it is) is the gaze that has become a stain (in the sense of a blind spot), almost literally or in the sense of a signpost. The other concern is the fact that since the world is what the other says it is, the world "as such" is repressed, or denaturalized (we will make the remote control be a car, make a woman say that she is our wife, etc.).

Regarding the gaze of the other, why not admit that in its "becoming a stain" (which indicates what the world "is"—and correspondingly what it is not: the remote control instead of the small car), there is already the action of a "signifierization?" The gaze as such—uncontrollable animal that it is, place of the "real" other in the sense that it escapes symbolization, a ball that moves unpredictably— becomes precisely the place of symbolization par excellence, a kind of black hole where all future symbolization is concentrated. I am merely explaining here what has been discovered in cognitive science laboratories[3] (which in turn seem to confirm Lacan's theses). The eyes are like the umbilicus of symbolization in the infant and the small child, a symbolization that seems to already be the product of a chiasmus—the source of social misunderstanding. When the adult sees, the child sees that they are looking; when the child looks at what the adult is looking at, they see. The *Spaltung* ("splitting") between vision and gaze is original, umbilical, and constitutive as such.

Revisiting the Seminar *The Object Relation* (Before Grasping What Emerges as New in the Seminar *Anxiety*)

The seminar *The Object Relation* begins by highlighting what Lacan had already developed in previous seminars, which in 1956 would take the form of a kind of duplication in reality; just as it was previously necessary for the psychoanalyst to differentiate the symbolic from the imaginary with his famous Z schema, it was now necessary to distinguish two different registers within reality itself by way of a "gap," or a *Spaltung* inherent in symbolized reality as such. Lacan starts from the idea that reality is what any definition of the object encounters as a stumbling block. What is an object in psychoanalysis? I have established that any definition of the object must be developed based on the primacy of the symbolic.

To introduce this notion of a duplication of reality generated by the symbolic, Lacan evokes the Freudian dichotomy of the reality principle and the pleasure principle, with all of its paradoxical implications. Indeed, pleasure is related to a state of rest, the desire to go back or to regain a state of balance, but it is also and above all a desire for excitation and the repetition of this excitation. The state of rest conceived by Freud is never zero; it is always >0. If language "mortifies," according to a well-established idea of Lacan's, it is also what makes things desirable, giving one a chance to recapture the pleasure that has been lost due to mortification–symbolization (the arbitrary and symbolic world); it allows for obtaining a "pleasure bonus," according to Freud's expression. The pleasure principle presupposes a way of circumventing reality while also constituting an "obstacle" to its realization. Furthermore, it is through this very detour around the obstacle that pleasure is fulfilled. There is therefore no pleasure, or "life," without constraint. Lacan states, "The word in German is *Lust*, with the ambiguous meaning that Freud underscores, both pleasure and yearning, which are indeed two things that can appear contradictory but which are no less efficaciously linked in experience.[4]"

But Lacan immediately connects this gap between rest and desire inherent in the living being to the gap that exists between the signifier and the signified. There is therefore a parallel and permanent superposition between two very different registers, that of the signified and that of the signifier. Here, we are merely revisiting the foundations of Lacanian theory and Lacan's reading of Freud. But what becomes immediately apparent is that this significant—and "energetic" gap, since it is at the origin of the drive—owes much to the theoretical foundations proposed by Lévi-Strauss in his preface to Marcel Mauss's 1950 work—it will be worthwhile to briefly revisit this.

The gap in question is nothing other than the differential perceived by de Saussure, but especially by Jakobson. What does this mean? It seems clear that Lévi-Strauss postulates the supremacy of the signifier over the world (and thus over the signified), but he also suggests that there is a kind of excess of the signifier over the signified, even if this does not seem to imply that the signifier has answers to everything at the level of what there is "to be signified.[5]" This is why Lévi-Strauss resorts to the notion of a floating signifier, for example, in the interpretation he

dedicates to the concept of mana. We will not be surprised to learn that, for someone like Lacan (but we should also add de Saussure), every signifier is floating.
Every signifier seizes the opportunity to fix a signified—but does it always suc-
ceed? Everything that has been said so far would indicate otherwise.

Let's address the preface written by the ethnologist for Marcel Mauss's book.
On the one hand, Lévi-Strauss advances this very well-known and commented
phrase: "Mauss still thinks it possible to develop a sociological theory of symbolism, whereas it is obvious that what is needed is a symbolic origin of society.[6]" The phrase indicates that everything in a given social system is concerned,
or determined, by the hegemony of the signifier or, as Marxist theorists would say,
by reification (everything, because it is assumed that nothing escapes language
and exchange). If we take the example of the gift, which Mauss considers a "total
social fact" involving all strata of society and all symbolic facts, we realize that the
gift is a signifying process independent of the exchanged object since most often
this object is something insignificant and, above all, useless. The object, by definition secondary, is determined by the signifier. On the other hand—and this may
be surprising—Lévi-Strauss considers not all individuals within a population to
have access to symbolic tools (marriage, filiation, gift). Entire segments of society
remain outside of the symbolic order; the author is thinking here of the insane, for
example, who remain outside of the system.

I would not be commenting on the introduction to Marcel Mauss written by
Lévi-Strauss if Lacan had not done so; my intention is to read Lacan. Lévi-Strauss
specifies that,

Any society at all is therefore comparable to a universe in which only discrete
masses are highly structured. So, in any society, it would be inevitable that a
percentage (itself variable) of individuals find themselves placed 'off system',
so to speak, or between two or more irreducible systems. The group seeks and
even requires of those individuals that they figuratively represent certain forms
of compromise which are not realizable on the collective plane; that they simulate imaginary transitions, embody incompatible syntheses.[7]

One might wonder why the anthropologist is interested in this aspect of exception to the symbolic rule, but upon closer inspection, we might ask, is it really an
exception to the rule or, on the contrary, isn't this exception precisely what gives
us a more complete vision of the configuration of the primacy of the symbolic? In
other words, these marginal elements do not enjoy all the symbolic advantages of
the system (marriage, gift), and yet they can be included in the symbolic system in
more than one way, so that it is the total rule that prevails, even for elements that
are always supposed to be outside the symbolized totality.

But there is more, because this implies that necessarily something escapes the
system, something that precisely indicates that the symbolic is there but that it
could, under certain conditions, no longer be there. As the author points out, "it

follows that no society is ever integrally and completely symbolic." The whole is not the totality, proof of which is the discovery of this other significant element called mana, a "do-it-all" signifier that works where there is no longer a signified, when the coverage of the signifier is no longer sufficient to signify a referent that has become a "minority" or that is "outside of the system." This residue that suddenly escapes from the signified is immediately included in the signifying system through mana.

Anxiety, or What Escapes the Symbolic Order

"*O que é este bicho vermelho?*" It is with this Portuguese phrase that Lévi-Strauss, in his famous *Introduction to the Work of Marcel Mauss*, explains the function of mana when he writes,

> Mauss quotes in the Sketch a very profound remark by Father Thavenet regarding the notion of manitou among the Algonquins: "it designates more particularly any being that does not yet have a common name, that is not familiar: a woman said she was afraid of a salamander. . . . Likewise, the first group of semi-civilised Tupi Kawahib Indians, with whose help we were to reach an unknown village of the tribe in 1938, admired the lengths of red flannel we presented to them and exclaimed: "O que é este bicho vermelho?" ("What is this red animal?"), which was neither evidence of primitive animism, nor the translation of an indigenous notion, but merely an idiomatic expression of the *falar cabóclo,* the rustic Portuguese of the interior of Brazil.[8]

This means that, unlike Mauss, Lévi-Strauss rejects the idea that things have a soul. Denying, however, the animist hypothesis in the case of mana, he attributes to it instead the function, as we know, of floating signifier. What thereby emerges is that this signifier appears where the symbolic universe is lacking, making an *Umheimlich* dimension appear to use the Freudian terminology. In other words, it emerges in the case of "any being that does not yet have a common name, that is not familiar". Let us remember that we started from the idea that the symbolic makes the world familiar. Thus, Marcel Hénaff points out that,

> mana is the name of everything that escapes knowledge, of what exceeds available explanations. It is the name of this gap or this inability to name (. . .) Lévi-Strauss proposes to include such terms (like 'thingy' or 'whatchamacallit' in French) in the notion of 'floating signifier,' an indeterminate signifier assigned to any unknown signified.[9]

It is no coincidence that Lacan revisits the notion of the *Unheimlich* ("the uncanny") when discussing anxiety in his 1962–1963 seminar. He introduces anxiety in direct relation to the lack of a signifier and to how the object's unrealization (its transformation into a signifier) is projected onto the image of that object, so it is projected onto the fact that any demand is illusory. Any response is a false response, an answer that fills the gap, or the void between the desired object and the obtained object. In absolute terms, one might suppose that the greater the difference between the symbolic (the gift, for example) and the object, the less we are in the realm of anxiety and conversely that once what we wanted has been obtained, the link between the object and its desire (thus the lack that makes it exist as a narcissistic object) can be put in peril. This is the moment of anxiety.

If Lacan wanted to emphasize this aspect of anxiety, it is both because it is a verifiable fact and because it is an ethical attitude (I will return to this point in the section on transference and the desire of the analyst). Therefore, it is necessary to start from the familiarity imposed by the primacy of the symbolic in order to detect its insufficiency, which gives rise to what is not symbolizable or what holds the place of the nonsymbolizable, namely anxiety. If we take the example of little Hans, Lacan's reading would consist in saying that there is a "red creature" (a salamander, an unclassified and unfamiliar being): the boy's erections. And the anxiety of the unfamiliar emerges at the place of this phobia that functions as a floating signifier. That is, to Lacan, if the father had been more "castrating," the erections would have been more familiar and the phobia consequently less necessary.

Indeed, a more in-depth reading of Lévi-Strauss's *Introduction to the Work of Mauss* is required. Lévi-Strauss criticizes Mauss and considers that the famous "Essay on the Gift" by the French sociologist was too imbued with ideas from another essay, written twenty years earlier, on magic.[10] Lévi-Strauss believes that Mauss puts too much faith in mana in the sense that the latter reduces mana to the attribution of a soul to all those things that remain "unclassified" by the symbolic when they in fact must be (hence the designation of mana, according to the structuralist's reading).

This is not at all what Mauss thinks; on the contrary, he interprets mana in the same way that Freud does the *Unheimlich*, namely as "foreign things,[11]" thereby relating this concept to animism. We can go even further: Freud relates mana to animism and therefore to what he describes as "the omnipotence of thoughts," thus evoking the famous case of the *Rat Man*. In other words, with the omnipotence of thoughts and so-called magical thinking, Freud would draw closer to Mauss and the fact that, indeed, there is something uncanny in certain objects or animals. Mauss rightly evokes the notion of animism, whereas Lévi-Strauss, by linking mana to the functioning of signifiers, might be throwing the baby out with the bathwater. If truth be told, this question is far more complex than indicated, since Freud himself rejects Jentsch's interpretation,[12] which he cites in his writing, according to which it would be the aspect of an automaton or something inanimate that gives the impression of the uncanny. Freud believes that it is something else, something "beyond," that produces the uncanny, even if he sometimes supports Jentsch's hypothesis (for example, "We have seen that a powerful effect of the uncanny is produced when things, images, or inanimate dolls come to life").[13]

It is clear that the theories of someone like Masahiro Mori—such as the famous "uncanny valley"—would precisely go in this direction.[14] Moreover, we know that Philippe Descola practices a rereading of symbolic thought, identifying "ontologies": animism, naturalism, totemism, and analogism.[15] He gives the example of a nuclear engineer who immerses himself in naturalistic (scientific) discourse but who, once his work is done, would avoid crossing paths with a black cat, thus revealing a resurgence of animism (and the omnipotence of thoughts, Freud would say). What I want to say is that all these considerations on "animism" lend importance to Mauss's observations, limit the theoretical Procrustean bed imposed by Lévi-Strauss, and allow us to reinstate the uncanny and anxiety—just as Lacan does in his 1963 seminar.[16] Yet this does not change the essence of Freud's demonstration, namely that it is when a part of the body seems dismembered, and therefore linked to castration, that the uncanny resurfaces; this is a corollary of Mauss's primary interpretation in the sense that it is when a part of the body seems to have a life of its own that it becomes uncanny. But here, just as Freud thinks of genital castration, we can think of the motif of the gaze and the eyes, both of which are very present, for example, in E.T.A. Hoffmann's "The Sandman."

In the Beginning Was the Symbolic

Since it is in the seminar on anxiety that Lacan eminently revisits the optical and structural effects of the "inverted bouquet," we must now dwell on a sort of rereading of the mirror stage. The paradox can be stated as follows: even if the original matrix is that of the imaginary register constituted by the mirror stage, this matrix can only be instituted from the gap introduced by the speaking being in and through the symbolic register, a gap that occurs very early, as early as two months of life. This would somewhat change Lacan's initial conclusion that it takes the moment of stabilization of Oedipus for the symbolic to reign.

The experimental data collected by Philippe Rochat and his team, for example, would place this primacy of the symbolic (and the object a that goes with it?) well before Oedipus, precisely at the end of the mirror stage. The symbolic must thus come first, while the imaginary is nothing other than a consequence of this first instance; even if the idea of familiarity may seem tinged with an imaginary dimension, the only familiarity that matters is the one granted to us by the symbolic register, which is connected to customary concern—what is isolated by Freud and what produces anxiety. On closer inspection, this is a predictable corollary: if our familiarity with the world—the world that is there, within our reach—is given to us through the symbolic, and if this symbolic takes the place of the world as such ("as such" meaning without the impact of the signifier, as is the case with autism), then this world as such (the bare world) is lost. We don't care about it, and this is how it can resurface in the form of anxiety.[17]

The moment when things begin to exist even though we do not require them as such is the moment of anxiety, and the same goes for anything unfamiliar that appears in our perception. What can appear in our perception is nothing less than a remnant of the Other's otherness, an otherness that is annihilated by the symbolic. In this regard, it is worth quoting a rather strange explanation from Lacan that nevertheless reveals the core of his thinking about the function of "object a":

> First off, you find A, the originative Other as locus of the signifier, and S, the subject as yet inexistent . . . with regard to the Other, the subject dependent upon this Other is inscribed as a quotient. . . . There is, in the sense of division, a remainder, a leftover. This remainder, this ultimate Other, this irrational entity, this proof, and the sole guarantee, when all is said and done, of the in the Other's otherness, is the a.[18]

This means that this a is the only thing that remains of the annihilated world, the one that is there before the being becomes a subject of the signifier. And it is also this a that can become a source of anxiety.

If the word is the "killing of the thing," it is because language already prepares us to know the world before we have access to it. The dimension of imaginary desire, ever-changing and fluctuating between all or nothing, is the one that can precisely combine the familiar and the uncanny, a univocal figure of the real as nonsymbolizable that obeys the primary system "in so far as the identity of perception is its rule.[19]" In this part of my work, I will attempt to grasp the following issue: even though the imaginary register comes to supplement the inherent gaps in the symbolic register, it can also be the means through which the necessary corollary of the familiar emerges, namely the uncanny. The imaginary comes to fill the referential opacity[20] to which we are subjected simply by being speaking beings—for the real referent is abolished as such—but it can, of course, fail in its task. We thus speak of the instability of the imaginary. The imaginary is the register through which Lacan will be able to introduce something other than the battery of signifiers (a notion through which he had carried out his return to Freud) into the clinic in the form of the fantasy.

The "Image of One's Own Body" and the Ego

It seems that Lacan's hypothesis in the 1930s was one of a continuity between the ego (and even the I) and the image of the body, in the sense that the reflected image is the image of the other, and that it almost has the status of a kind of prosthesis, an almost artificial element. Thus, and essentially, the image of the body can become unfamiliar or even unsettling due to a lack of self-recognition (consider the example found, especially in normal people, of depersonalization). Conversely, the image of the other's body can be invested as if it were familiar. In a certain sense, it is through the imaginary that one can grasp the dimension of the object a's function; indeed, this imaginary is dependent on the image—an image strictly dependent upon on a totality or a gestalt that gives it coherence—because if one considers it in each of its parts, the whole risks disintegrating, even if only for a brief moment.

The total form takes precedence over the sum of its parts, but it can also be weakened in its totality, as evidenced by the experiments conducted in laboratories by gestalt theory over the past decades. The vision in the mirror as an imaginary totality is made so that it cannot be decomposed into its parts without risking the breakdown of its coherence in its entirety. The subjective effects produced by this breakdown are well-known (depersonalization, strange self-perception, uncanny strangeness, etc.).

I want to explore the imaginary register and its relations with the concept of object a. If one is serious, one should start by wondering why something called the image of the body can even exist. Lacan gives a status to the body that is compatible with the ego, so compatible that it becomes indistinguishable from it. Body and ego are continuous.

Such an assertion is not self-evident; why indeed should the image of the body be so important? If the symbolic institutes a gap or a *Spaltung* in the living being so that the relationship with oneself is never immediate, it is up to the imaginary to fill the gap. I have already shown in my remarks on the mirror stage that the image of oneself cannot be immediate either; as we have seen with Lacan and Baron-Cohen, the image of the body as the perceiving self sees it places the living being on the one hand in an external position with respect to himself (because he sees himself as if he, the being, were an other); on the other hand, this image is his most present being, the most radically version of himself (or at least it claims to be). The image therefore has a paradoxical, unstable status, even if this instability proves that it is the dimension of the other that prevails, that dominates. In a sense, this image that I see reflected is already the other. Why? For a very simple reason: it is perceived from the perspective of this other, with the pair of eyes of the other drawn by Baron-Cohen in his optical schema. The body as such is already the effect of the murder of the thing, as is any object in the socialized world.

But we must go further: perception of oneself—of one's own body—is no more immediate. It should probably be specified that the body in question, one's own body, can only be appropriated by the living being through the symbolic. This appropriation facilitates the almost intuitive apprehension of the image of oneself, in the assumption, as Lacan would say, of one's own image—indeed, it is strange that this assumption is taken for granted, that no one hesitates to consider their own image as precisely their image. The ease with which this occurs can produce moments of strangeness, of failed acts in front of the image that make us perceive this other dimension of the image—not some metaphysical beyond but, on the contrary, the very concrete here-and-now of the image that, like any other daily object, is in reality impregnated with social usage, with the function that we willingly give it. This almost artificial aspect is even perceptible through the testing of the reality of this image, in a kind of daily experimentation that anyone can engage in without difficulty. If one wants to perform some movements on the posterior part of one's body (combing one's hair or another movement) using one's reflected image in the mirror rather than doing it "by heart," one easily loses control of one's gesture;

even though it has been given to us by exteroception, our proprioceptive mastery is more important if we do not rely on the exteroceptive image.

Indeed, one can decline the body according to the three Lacanian registers, and one will find that each register is a more or less incomplete entity, even artificial. The imaginary body is never entirely "capturable," visually graspable by the living being (even if our image is captured by different devices, there will always be a kind of "blind spot" that escapes us in our visual perception of ourselves, a perception that generally exists only when reflected in a flat mirror). It is enough to stand in front of a mirror and make some gestures intended to modify our customary optical perception—adding another mirror, for example—in order to see our perception change; so much for the imaginary register. Through social rules, the body is also subject to symbolic devices, regimes, gendered codes, hygienic norms, and "techniques of the body," which govern sex, gender, death, birth, health, etc. In this regard, it is worth reconsidering a remark by Lévi-Strauss that for him, the grip of the symbolic goes so far that, for him, even the thresholds of bodily and emotional excitability are culture-dependent. He does not think, however, upon reflection, that these affects are precisely what touch the edges of the symbolic ("the 'unrealizable' effort, the 'intolerable' pain, the 'unheard-of' pleasure"). Thus, finally, with regard to the register of the real, there are "other reals"; this is the case with anxiety and other affects that lie beyond the imaginary body and symbolic constraints.

In a sense, it is not even necessary for a body to have an image; therefore, it is not necessary for there to be a body either, if in certain respects the body can be reduced to its image—the organism should suffice as a biological envelope. It is unnecessary to respond that in animals' body image has a crucial function because, as everyone knows, it is in no way the image of an animal's "own" body but rather that of its congeners. Thus, it is not certain that there is a subjectivation of the body in animals.[21]

But upon closer examination, is there really a subjectivation in humans? To what extent does the image the child sees reflected on a surface imply that it corresponds to any such "own body"? Is the body not, in reality, perfectly external? Do we not ultimately content ourselves with the image that others reflect back to us? Let us return to the Baron-Cohen/Lacan schema: to symbolically incorporate the world and its objects (including one's own body), we need to unrealize and signifierize it. If one's own body is signifierized, we do not see it as such but see it through what we are allowed to see—through the symbolic prism. Through this question, we can easily grasp the cleavage implied by the mirror image, which Lacan explained by his optical schema: the image we see, which contains a certain imaginary precariousness, does not necessarily correspond to the image we want to see (I deliberately use the impersonal "we" to emphasize the impersonal nature of this experience, an experience that does not come from the self). Lacan's famous idea that the subject sees itself "from the other" does not require an external gaze as such; the subject sees itself as if it were itself that external gaze: it "is" that "other."

After all, shouldn't Lacan have concluded that there is no such thing as one's own body since it is in continuity with the status he gives to the self, a self that is not sufficient to account for anything of the being that Lacan calls subject, a product of the symbolic *Spaltung*? The self is, on the contrary, in continuity both with respect to the proprio- and interoceptive bodily experience and with respect to the exteriority assumed by the symbolic register from the moment it annihilates the world and the body with it. We know that Lacan places the body in a certain relationship of concordance (better yet, of continuity thanks to the Möbius strip experiment, for example) with what is most intimate in the living being (most intimate because, precisely, it is little or not at all represented by the symbolic, which codifies everything within its reach) and what is exterior to the living being—that most "extimate" exterior marginalized by the same symbolic register, a dimension that, in Lacan, has some salutary connotations (this symbolic dimension is deficient in psychosis, for example).

When it comes to what is most intimate with regard to the body, Lacan speaks of a "libidinal reserve"; for what is most exterior, he will consider the supposition of a function, the object a function in the sense that it would align with the libidinal reserve of the drive. What is most intimate regarding the body (think, for example, of the experience of orgasm) has as its correlate what is most exterior to the living being, something thought to be an object of desire. What would be the image projected in the mirror of an orgasm? What is the visual form of the orgasm as such, beyond its phallicized image, as an interoceptive bodily experience? This led Lacan to say that it is the orgasm that masks anxiety.[22]

Familiarity, Not "Fragmentation"

For Lacan, the history of the human being begins with the mirror stage, with a body. There is a body rooted in the biological, except that our author assumes that due to a kind of neurophysiological immaturity, the body is "fragmented[23]" in such a way that it is also inhabited by a distress that is its own. This bodily fragmentation, both subjective and objective, is due to a biological prematuration specific to humans, a notion that Lacan borrowed from the Dutch naturalist L. Bolk. Needless to say, the reference was (and still is) outdated, but it nevertheless has the merit of clarifying how the human being takes its first steps in the world, steps for which it must at the very least be assisted. This objective fact therefore means that from the outset, the infant is confronted with suffering, a suffering inherent to the state of being alive. Thus, if we take the notion of stress as an example, we will see that it presents itself as an irreducible necessity, a quasi-transcendental in the sense that there could be no organism without an inherent and necessary amount of stress for its survival (that is, for life). And, mutatis mutandis, there is no body without stress and, therefore, without distress (*Hilflosigkeit*). The organism has a body in the sense of a bodily envelope. The question then becomes: is this envelope sufficient to bear the distress?

The Body Not Reduced to the Symbolic: On Jouissance

We have seen that the symbolic register alone would not suffice to give consistency to the living being and that it must be endowed with a sort of ipseity—a sameness—to the point that without this notion of body image, the mind would have a tendency to function without limits, a brain in a vat. I am aware that by mentioning a "sameness," I am departing from Lacanian vocabulary, but it must be acknowledged that even if this body belongs to the other, we take it as our own. The symbolic gives consistency to the world, it signifierizes it, but it should be obvious that the body cannot be just an object among others.

If we revisit Freud's thesis developed in *Beyond the Pleasure Principle,* we are reminded that there is no adequate envelope for the drive. This thesis results in a constant dehiscence between disease and its remedy. The disease: the "death drive"; the remedy: the egoic envelope and the "pleasure principle," which as best as it can regulates this drive by making it compatible with the symbolic because there is a need to alleviate distress at its lowest level. At the same time, though, it is impossible to reach zero desire; as I have already indicated, the lowest possible level of displeasure is >0, or greater than zero (Lacan's libidinal reserve). This permanent gradient >0 is called the "death drive," or simply drive (since every drive is a death drive),[24] and we can already venture to say that this >0 is related to the function of the object a.

My story could end here: "original castration" refers to the fact that displeasure will always be greater than 0; it is the lowest possible level: even after an infant feeds or after the most satisfying sexual act, they sleep, but they do not have peace: >0. This is the origin of the paradox that lack translates into excess: after coupling or feeding, the lack persists and exceeds any imagined or expected fulfillment. Of course, one could always refute this Freudian observation and argue that it cannot be synchronic (while one is satisfied one is, by definition, not dissatisfied), but only diachronic (after satisfaction, there will at some point be a new dissatisfaction for biological reasons). What interests us here, beyond biological rhythms, is the subjectivation of these alternations between satisfaction and dissatisfaction. This is why the concept of jouissance, which is at least ambiguous in Lacan, can be defined (in one of its meanings) as "a composed formula encompassing the two terms of the Freudian binarism, libido and the death drive.[25]"

This alternation between the imaginary satisfaction of desire linked to an object and the fundamental dissatisfaction determined by the metonymic nature of desire makes the montage around an object that will have an excessive emotional charge—excessive if we think of the charge it will no longer have after the satisfaction associated with it. This alternation must also be accounted for in the function of the object a, well beyond the object of desire, which is not permanent as such. To put it succinctly, there is a direct correlation between the bodily tension that exceeds the bodily envelope and the image of the object: the object of desire, which in one way or another will always be inadequate, all the more so since it is supposed to satisfy the living being, the drive, and desire at the same time.

The Doubling of the Image

The function of the object a translates into a kind of stumbling point, especially in the image of one's own body; this is essentially Lacan's thesis. Wallon, whom I have already cited, is interested in the gesture of turning the head (what we would call today "joint attention"), which allows us to take into account what he calls a kind of "doubling" of the child in front of his own image; this doubling generally occurs at a very precise moment in the symbolization of the world and the construction of the child's personality. In front of the mirror, contrary to what Lacan asserts, as I have already pointed out, the child does not just laugh (or jubilate); he can also experience a sort of "confusion[26]" or moments of perplexity in which he does not know what corresponds to a reflected image and what pertains to reality.

This doubling of the child in front of his image, described by Wallon, clearly shows the necessity of on the one hand the reflected image (of the child) or of other objects and on the other, in a second moment, the "real" objects, starting with the child's body and the bodies of others. If the child then engages in the gesture of turning toward the other, it is because between the image and the real object that is reflected in it, something does not fit. It is as if, on one side or the other, something is lost—something that is not entirely absorbed by the image and its symbolization.

Lacan writes in "The Mirror Stage,"

> As I myself have shown, human knowledge is more independent than animal knowledge from the force field of desire because of the social dialectic that structures human knowledge as paranoiac; but what limits it is the "scant reality" surrealistic unsatisfaction denounces therein. These reflections lead me to recognize in the spatial capture manifested by the mirror stage, the effect in man, even prior to this social dialectic, of an organic inadequacy of his natural reality—assuming we can give some meaning to the word "nature.[27]"

What should we make of this statement? First of all, there is a preponderance of the imaginary preceding any dialecticization of signifiers. This proposition may seem banal, but it implies that the imago in question precedes any subjective experience of entering language. Moreover, the invention of the word *prémanent* ("prior"), which does not exist as such in the French language, should draw our attention to Lacan's desire to give form to a phenomenon that escapes any subjective experience. In other words, one might suppose that this word *prémanent*, invented by Lacan to account for the specular clinic, refers to everything that is innate—if we follow the innatist biologists—and to all that is, is prior to any subjective dialectic.

This assumption may alarm adherents of the dialectic, of the symbolic, who typically reject any naturalistic or biological approach. These are, however, the facts from which Lacan begins in "Mirror Stage." It is not that I want to portray the young Lacan (let us recall that the 1936 text was rewritten in 1949 and slightly revised again in 1966) as a defender of innateness; what I am trying to prove is that something owes much to this instance of the primordial imaginary can later escape the symbolic register since it is active long before symbolic primacy. Along the lines of this assertion, a few lines later, we read, "Let us note in passing that this datum [the famous 'specific prematurity of birth in humans'] is recognized as such by embryologists, under the term fetalization, to determine the prevalence of the so-called superior apparatuses of the neuraxis and especially of this cortex, which psycho-surgical interventions will lead us to conceive as the intra-organic mirror.[28]" If an innate phenomenon appears before its "cause"—a dialectical cause—and seems to persist once this cause has been introduced, then it is an irreducible predisposition. The word "mirror" in the expression "intra-organic mirror," even if it is put forth critically, clearly suggests that the mirror is already there before the mirror of the Other. If we were to speak Wallon's language, we would say that the proprioceptive is there before the extroceptive projects its decisive impact.

"There Is No Other of the Other," the Prerequisites of Language, and the Libidinal Reserve

One has often heard Lacan's saying, "There is no Other of the Other,[29]" but like any saying, it is opaque until we find an example to which to apply it. Let us reconsider here what cognitive psychology calls the "prerequisites of language.[30]" Given that what matters for incorporating language and for speaking is something that precedes language (prerequisites such as joint attention and imitation) and that it is not language itself, we can wonder what the relationship would be between these two instances: language and the prerequisites of language.

What do we mean by the prerequisites of language? I have described that long before a child begins to speak, they communicate with their gaze. This gaze of course involves vision but also and especially what this vision can see: notably, the gaze of others. The gaze of the other presents, very early on, a surprising characteristic: unlike furniture and other objects in the world, it has a life of its own; it is undoubtedly a minimal parameter to which the very young baby, the infant, can (and must) cling. Baron-Cohen, who emphasizes the importance of eyes, notes how they are as such "unpredictable" for the speaking being: "in real life, gaze direction shifts rapidly and in partially unpredictable sequences.[31]"

In autism, for example, this can pose a problem because it is a common trait that autistic persons are averse to eye contact, to the gaze of others. It is also interesting that the Anglo-Saxon author begins his sentence by referring to "real life"—in other words, everyday life—which one can occasionally find suddenly, in front of the mirror or when faced with the gestures of others who disconcert us, a vitality that is not programmed or for which we do not necessarily have the answers. This vitality of the gaze of others is what leads us into the world, allowing us to follow, when possible, the direction of the gaze (and this is why Baron-Cohen speaks of the gaze direction detector: in the unpredictability of the other, we seek to detect a meaning, a direction, a goal, or an intention that is not ambiguous). It is also quite amusing that the cognitivist calls the attraction to the gaze of the other a gaze detector, to the point where one might wonder "who detects whom?" I will come back to this.

The prerequisites of language open on to the symbolization of the world, create meaning, and give functionality to things. They are ultimately born of the unpredictable, the contingent; they are themselves irrefutable proof of the existence of contingency in the speaking being. Joint or shared attention begins to establish itself around the fourth or fifth month and will subsequently be a sine qua non condition for the existence of language, particularly in terms of receptive language, that is, understanding.

The legitimate question to ask is: does this prerequisite of speech (the gaze of others that gives meaning) already belong to language? When we think about the fact that the other gives us a sense of things, of ourselves, and of our image, and that this constitutes a kind of alienation from the other (their desire, their meanings, their intentions)—which reflects a reified version of reality back to us—we might think that this "alienation" will later require some sort of separation so that we can go beyond what the other signifies to us. Were this to be true, it is difficult to imagine what this separation would comprise. Traumas? Contingent moments? Bodily experiences that would give a different meaning to what we had received as signification?

If there is a separation, it is already operated and operative by the very fact of being guided by the contingent gaze of the other. The fact that one "passes" from a primary to a secondary intersubjectivity—that is, from an immediate relationship to the other (eye to eye) to a transition toward other objects of sharing and common interest—already implies a separation from the gaze (and therefore from the other). The mere fact of being able to rely on this gaze is already a separation insofar as it prepares us for contingency—once again, autism can serve as a compass for us, by negation: there is no place for contingency, no preparation for the "referential opacity" that the symbolic register, as Lacan conceives it (the signifier as arbitrary), requires.

The question then is: do the prerequisites of language belong to language as such? Answering in the negative does not provide a sufficient response. How can one signify the world without already "signifying" the prerequisite that will signify the world? And if one answers positively, this does not satisfy us either, because if the prerequisite of language already belongs to language, then it is useless to call it a prerequisite—it is already part of language. One should apply Russell's paradox here;[32] we know that this paradox was criticized by logicians (by the very same Russell, in fact, in creating "type theory"), precisely because it is a theory created based on a referential opacity. Regardless, Lacan referred to it, and that is what interests us. The paradox can be applied to the status of the object a, as it showed how the object a was more of a function than an object.

Thus, in both cases, the concept of the prerequisite of language is itself paradoxical. Why dwell on this aspect, which may seem too theoretical and clinically unimportant? Because this place, this function is, in a way, already external, due to its paradoxical nature and to the nature of language as such, which means here that the living being must reify itself and must pass through the paths of the other, of speech, and of the symbolic. The path of desire as such goes beyond the subject–object relationship and requires something else, a third instance, like the one Lacan assigns to the signifier. This external, third function—which is situated in the establishment of the symbolic—is related to the function of the object a such that this function both is and is not the subject, is both internal and external at the same time. The function of the object a then becomes a "between" language and the prerequisites of the symbolic.

I have not forgotten, however, that we are trying to determine the status of the object a in the imaginary register. What impact could the imaginary capture we have studied so far have after the living being's introduction into the "social dialectic," according to Lacan's expression in "The Mirror Stage"? What remains of this decisive moment of the formation of the I for the living being after it enters the symbolic register? It is in *Anxiety* (1962) that Lacan revisits the mirror stage to define the narcissistic object and distinguish what escapes it, which implies two kinds of objects: those that "are shared" and those that "are not shared,[33]" meaning those that do not enter into exchange, into the social dialectic.

From Winnicott to Lacan and Back

It is worth recalling here the importance Donald Winnicott's concepts of the transitional object and the more general transitional phenomenon[34] had for Lacan. It is well-known that Lacan affirmed that his object a is Winnicott's transitional object,[35] but he also stated that, "We were the first to exactly situate the theoretical importance of the so-called transitional object, isolated as a clinical trait by Winnicott.[36]" And further,

It is undoubtedly because of this lack of temperament that Winnicott believed he had to contribute his own self to it. But also to receive this transitional object from the more distant hands of the child, which we must return here since it is from him that we first formulated objet a.[37]

These three quotations are coherent with one another in the sense that they indicate a debt to the English psychoanalyst, even if the second implies a strange order of priority: "we were the first to exactly situate the theoretical importance of the so-called transitional object." One can also read, "it is from him [the transitional object] that we first formulated objet a." It is as if there were a transitional theoretical space between the two authors, or more precisely, from Lacan to Winnicott, in which it is no longer clear to whom the discovery belongs. What interests me here is understanding how the transitional object can shed light on Lacan's objet a.

What is the transitional object? One must first think in terms of space: in the intersubjective space between the mother and the child, something appears that is neither one nor the other—this is the transitional phenomenon. It is a place of both sharing and differentiation; within this space some object appears (a piece of wool, cloth, or blanket) that is not the self (not-me), nor the other. Winnicott writes, "When symbolism is employed the infant is already clearly distinguishing between fantasy and fact, between inner objects and external objects.[38]" It is thus through the symbolic that something that seems to occur between the child and the other (the mother, the adult) is transferred to objects that I will call "whatever" objects. One can again cite Winnicott to this effect:

> I have introduced the terms 'transitional objects' and 'transitional phenomena' for designation of the intermediate area of experience, between the thumb and the teddy bear, between the oral erotism and the true object-relationship, between primary creative activity and projection of what has already been introjected, between primary unawareness of indebtedness and the acknowledgement of indebtedness.[39]

It is surprising for Lacan's readers to read the word "debt" (indebtedness) from the British author's pen because it is indeed a debt that the child will have toward the other insofar as it is through him that he is introduced into the symbolic world, a world where one lives on credit, so to speak. The author enlightens us about the nature of the object in question when he declares,

> It is true that the piece of blanket (or whatever it is) is symbolical of some part-object, such as the breast. Nevertheless, the point of it is not its symbolic value so much as its actuality. Its not being the breast (or the mother), although real, is as important as the fact that it stands for the breast (or mother).[40]

Let us translate this into Lacanian language: it doesn't matter that the transitional object is symbolic of a partial object (and thus imaginary); what matters is that it takes a certain place ("that it is not the breast") and therefore exists through the symbolic register. As object, it is the killing of the thing (the breast). If one wanted to go further, one could suppose that in this single paragraph, I have declined Lacan's three registers insofar as the relation to the breast (oral erotism) reveals the implication of the real as the register corresponding to the silence of drives.[41] To put it another way, transitional phenomena should be situated in Baron-Cohen's schema in the space between the child and the adult, and transitional objects in the space that forms between the child and the "window" (the square) of the world where barely symbolized objects appear.

The Simplified Schema

Let us therefore try to situate our mirror stage within the Lacanian coordinates of the 1960s, at a time when Lacan attempts to make his audience understand this new real dimension of the object, the objet a. It is indeed a dimension of the object, which is why Lacan prefers to speak of "the status of what I initially designated by the letter a."

It is not certain that he necessarily speaks of an objet a. Let's revisit his reflection from the December 5, 1962, session where, in Chapter IV, entitled "Beyond Castration Anxiety" by J.-A. Miller, Lacan draws a sort of "simplified diagram" of the inverted bouquet.[42] Regarding this diagram, Lacan clarifies, "At this place, *i'(a)*, in the Other, in the locus of the Other, an image emerges that is merely the reflection of ourselves. It's authenticated by the Other, but it's already problematic, fallacious even.[43]"

Why does Lacan emphasize the "merely reflected" aspect of this image? Moreover, we notice that he asserts something that aligns with Wallon's concept of doubling: even authenticated by the Other, the image is problematic (as we have seen elsewhere, Rochat thinks that moments of confusion, typical in young children, can resurface in adults). Why, then, consider that this image is "merely reflected"? It would have sufficed to assert that it is reflected, but since it is already framed by the Other, that is, by permutation (Wallon's turning gesture and therefore, shared attention), it is no longer a simple imaginary capture, as is the case in the initial phase of the mirror stage emphasized pertinently by Wallon.

The child has "turned around" (checking back), so that we are no longer in a first logical time, if I may put it that way. Since the image has been authenticated by the Other, the symbolic is there, and the child is no longer "alone." Lacan continues, "It is authenticated by the Other, but already problematic, even fallacious." Indeed, the image wouldn't be "problematic" without the permutation, without the "nutation of the head." It becomes problematic precisely because we already have a subjective instance other than that of the total imaginary capture proposed in the mirror stage. And if this image is problematic, it is because it is fallacious; it doesn't occur naturally and is not identical to itself, and even less so to the being it is supposed to represent. It is the reflected image, but it might also not be. The entire issue of the experience of the double is condensed here into a single sentence insofar as this double is never an exact duplicate, or a point-by-point copy of the original.

What is this 'simplified diagram' that appears in the seminar on anxiety? Why does it need to be simplified? In this seminar, Lacan spoke about a kind of ideal of simplicity, a form of minimalism proper to science. If this diagram is simplified, it is with respect to the one that is not—namely, the diagram of the inverted bouquet introduced by Lacan at the beginning of his teaching in 1954 and later revisited in his article "Remarks on Daniel Lagache's Presentation." So, what exactly is simplified? What reduction does Lacan operate with this new optical diagram? We quickly notice that the narcissistic image is missing. More precisely, everything related to the image is absent; the diagram is simplified for the simple reason that it is no longer "optical," that it no longer refers solely to the imaginary. And for good reason, as it attempts to capture what is "nonspecularizable" in any image (the famous libidinal reserve [see Figure 2.1], which is related to the erogenous rim). The second missing element is the eye, a crucial point in the classic diagram of the *Ecrits*; here we only find the "S" of the subject. The simplified diagram is the diagram of the subject and its lack: $(-\phi)$. It is as if only the living being confronted with the Other remains, embodied by the mirror (but we could also forget this mirror and leave only the "A") whose result is nothing other than $(-\phi)$.

In the November 28, 1962, session of the seminar on anxiety, there is an explicit reference to the classic diagram from "Remarks on Daniel Lagache's Presentation."

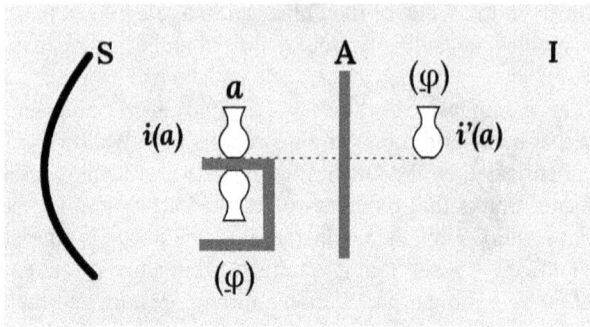

Figure 2.1 The Simplified Schema.

The diagram itself is not commented on, and Lacan prefers to save this explanation. However, there are traces of another diagram which will not be included in the published edition of the seminar.[44]

The lower part of simplified schema 1 represents the body of the subject, while in the same place, symmetrically, we have the "image of the other" but which does not contain our body. We are therefore given the image and the mirror insofar as the image of the other could just as well be the self-image (which will never be an exact double); it could also just as well be the image of one's partner, for example. The lower part of the diagram is problematic: where the "flowers" from the left-hand diagram were reflected in the right-hand mirror, we now find in the mirror, or more precisely, through the filter of the Other ("A" instead of the mirror), the image of the other that we lack: that is, the image of the other insofar as it is desirable but does not correspond to the libidinal reserve of the one's own body. In the upper part of the diagram, however, everything seems to flow naturally; here we see the image as it is desired, without incompleteness.

I would venture to say that Lacan simplified his diagram by complexifying it—that is, by adding the image of the other rather than that of one's own body from the mirror stage, which is the primitive diagram (1954–1960). I would go even further: in the place of the other (on the right), Lacan situated the square that Baron-Cohen would draw thirty years later, representing both the image of the world and the image of the other. And in this image of the other, where we should find the object that is to be sought in the other's desire, we find only the image of the other—a fallacious image since it is informed by the trait that desire grants it, the desire (of the other's gaze) that makes the remote control a little car (or makes a woman beautiful).

In one of his texts, Freud asks how it is that the lover does not see the loved one's cavities; instead of the cavities, there is a -ϕ, so that only i(a), the idealized image, remains. This matrix could be explained differently still, with the example of the child's play: image 1 is the real "little car" or "libidinal reserve"; image 2 is nothing more than the miserable, discarded, broken remote control left by the parents.

Does this prevent one from playing little car with the remote control? Far from it: it is -ϕ, the emptying out of the real object (the remote control), that creates i(a), the little car that is not. We approach the remote control with a repressed libidinal reserve—the image engraved in the mind by the little car once seen in the toy store window. This, in a nutshell, is Freud's theory of indestructible unconscious desire and also, incidentally, what doesn't work for the autistic person (again, Lacan will say that Dick doesn't know how to play: "this child does not play").

The Lack, Source of Repetition

One does not therefore really find in the other an "image" of our drive (and this is why Lacan notes -ϕ), otherwise they would either be mad or flirting with a kind of uncanniness. This is why Lacan continues his remarks with the following words, which I would like to emphasize: "This image is characterized by a lack, that is, by the fact that what is called upon there is unable to appear there.[45]" On this point, it is enough to recall the Fort-Da game described by Freud in the sense that what is called to appear there (let's say the mother) not only will not appear but has already well and truly disappeared through the very creation of the Fort-Da device. Moreover, it is in his rereading of Fort-Da in relation to the object a that Lacan evokes Wallon in order to explain that what the subject represents through a primary signifier (S1) necessarily implies a loss, a lost object as such, which ensures a point-by-point noncorrespondence between the lost object and the signifier that stands in the place of this loss.

The simplified diagram found on page 44 of *Anxiety* is therefore an optical diagram "without flowers" where one must content oneself with the image of the other—that is to say, with a variant of one's own image, where the object of desire is indeed present yet can in no way replace what drives us to move toward this image ("what is called there cannot appear"). It is certainly this drive that justifies movements of desire toward the other and not the other as such. It is therefore not surprising that Lacan ascribes great importance to the Fort-Da game observed by Freud when discussing repetition and its relationship to the object a. On one hand, in the child's game, we are not far from what I mentioned earlier regarding the remote control: the reel, found in relation to the socialized other—the mother in this case—is already linked to a first form of symbolization. On the other hand, if Wallon is called here as a theoretical witness, it is precisely in relation to the possibility of making an absence present. If we take the example of the gesture of turning toward the adult, of shared attention, we will see that there is already a loss, that there is already a sort of "Fort-Da" in the turning gesture; the child is already playing with the absence of the other, and the fact that he turns around indicates that this other could also no longer be there. Lacan explains,

> Wallon stresses that the child does not immediately watch the door through
> which his mother has disappeared, thus indicating that he expects to see her

return through it, but that his vigilance was aroused earlier, at the very point she left him, at the point she moved away from him.[46]

It is therefore already the case that "what is called upon there is unable to appear there,[47]" if only because something else has already been summoned: the reel, or the "remote control." This is how we can understand that "this bobbin . . . is a little something of the subject that detaches while still being very much his own, still retained.[48]" Again, we have Winnicott to thank.

As a result of this "transitional" space, we have a back-and-forth movement where one misses the target but derives satisfaction from it:

> On one hand, there is the reserve that can't be grasped in the imaginary, even though it is linked to an organ, which, thank goodness, is still perfectly grasp-able, this instrument which will all the same have to go into action from time for the satisfaction of desire, the phallus. On the other hand, there is the *a*, which is this remainder, this residue, this object whose status escapes the status of the object derived from the specular image, that is, the laws of transcendental aesthetics. All confusion has swept into analytic theory because its status is so hard to spell out.[49]

On one side—on the side of one's own body—there is the libido, that is, the penis; on the other side there is a, or that which is not seen through the "laws of transcenden-tal aesthetics," a statement through which one can perhaps understand the following phrase from Lacan: "he looks at himself, I would say, in his sexual member.[50]"

Undoubtedly, this erect penis reflected in the mirror—what the *Rat Man* exhibited only to then undergo the sanction of the father's gaze—is worthy because it is what looks at the penis-bearer, not because of what it is as a sexual attribute. Where the *Rat Man* thought he was seeing, he was in fact being looked at, as evi-denced by the sanction of the father's gaze that was to appear on the other side of the door (as if one were to say "on the other side of the mirror"). If Lacan's remark about Wallon ("thus indicating that he expects to see her return through it . . . at the very point she left him, at the point she moved away from him) makes sense, it is because this vanishing point—this point where there is a qualitative "leap" ("the game of leap")—is already symbolized; it is already a signifier of the other and, somewhere, it also makes present the gaze of the world—its mask.

The Object a Is Brilliant

One must thus call what inhabits our body to our own detriment the drive; as a result of this inhabiting, the drive is dislocated from the ego and, where appropri-ate, sends back to this ego an image that is foreign to it. The libidinal reserve thus constitutes nothing less than the life within us, a life so alive that we want nothing to do with it. It becomes, moreover, the element to be repressed, so that this life has an acceptable image in a mirror or corresponds to the proper name of the one who bears it. One might call this life that escapes us "brilliant," as Giorgio Agamben writes in one of his texts:

> Everything is us that is impersonal is genial. The force that pushes the blood, through our veins or that plunges us into sleep, the unknown power in our body that gently regulates and distributes its warmth or that relaxes or contract the fibers or our muscles—that too is genial. It is Genius that we obscurely sense in the intimacy of our physiological life, where the closest is the most foreign and the most impersonal, where the most intimate is the most distant and least controllable. . . . Living with Genius means, in this sense, living in the intimacy of a strange being, remaining constantly in relation to a zone of nonconsciousness. But this zone of nonconsciousness is not repression; it does not shift or displace an experience of consciousness to the unconscious.[51]

Agamben's negation should be treated as what it is: a negation. And yet, since every negation implies an affirmation—as much for Freud as for logicians[52]—he refutes psychoanalysis but thereby points to it as the obligatory reference when it comes to the brilliance of the drives. That being said, what interests me here primarily is the way Agamben presents this tension between the drive and the ego, to put it bluntly. The philosopher opposes the ego to Genius—that is, to the body as being necessarily constituted of borders that control Genius without being able to confine it to one precise border; one can sense a glimmer of what Lacan calls the object a beyond even the erogenous rim. This erogenous rim can only be satisfied by matter and by the signifying qualities that accompany it. Again, Agamben writes,

> One writes to become impersonal, to become brilliant, and yet, in writing, we individuate ourselves as the author of this or that work, we distance ourselves from Genius, which can never take the form of an Ego, and even less that of an author. . . . It may happen then that the repressed impersonal resurfaces in the form of symptoms. . . . In the face of Genius, no one is great; we are all equally small.[53]

"Small a's," we might say, as much as the libidinal reserve can serve their greatness as well as their decline. It is clear that Agamben's Freudian negation (Genius is not what pertains to the unconscious) becomes fruitful (the repressed impersonal that is Genius can return in the form of symptoms). I can only give the final word to the philosopher, who recognizes the impersonal species he calls "voice" as what can make us speak in the name of an unconscious:

> But some [men] are unconscious enough to let themselves be shaken and crossed by it to the point where they will fall apart. Others, more serious but less

fortunate, refuse to personalize the impersonal, to lend their lips to a voice that does not belong to them.[54]

Genius and the Mirror

Lacan continues to develop his argument about the specular image, an image that is fundamentally different from that of the living being: "it [the image of the other] orients and polarizes desire, it has a captation function for it. Desire is not only veiled there [this dimension is characteristic of unconscious desire, as introduced by Freud], but essentially related to an absence."

Thus far, we are in the Freudian domain—namely that of the lost object, as described in the *Project for a Scientific Psychology*. This is the negative dimension of the object, negative since it is by definition lost. But Lacan adds a nuance, or a positive dimension, which is that of "a," without which all the discourse he has just begun would have no significant bearing: "this absence is also the possibility of an appearance, which is controlled by a presence that lies elsewhere. . . . As I've indicated to you, the presence in question is that of the *a*.[55]" Those familiar with Lacan's texts cannot remain indifferent to the "elsewhere" and the "from where" in this quotation. The point from which one "sees oneself as lovable"—a point concealed from the mirror image—will no longer be a point by point correspondence with itself (which would be the territory of the ego), but rather a place that corresponds to Lacan's conception of the ego ideal. The missing point is where one "gets lost" by turning toward the ego ideal; starting from this turn, there is no longer a correspondence between the ego (i(a)) and the ego, and even less so between its own image and the one it finds in the mirror. In the phenomenon of love, moreover, one will lose oneself in a radical way. If the specular correspondence is not total—because one is captivated by a presence that is both elsewhere and is unreachable—then the key point that "captivates" and sequesters desire is, by definition, nonspecularizable, which is why we will find $(-\phi)$ at its place. Lacan continues,

> At this place of lack where something can appear, las time I put last, in brackets, the sign $(-\phi)$. This indicates for you that there emerges here a relationship with the libidinal reserve, namely, with that something that doesn't get projected, doesn't get invested in, at the level of the specular image, which is irreducible, fort the reason that it remains profoundly invested at the level of one's body, the level of primary narcissism, of what is called autoerotism, an autistic jouissance.[56]

In other words, Lacan clearly states that the image as such—that of the object of desire—is nothing without what the individual finds anew from their libidinal reserve, which the symbolic locates in the place of the other. This libidinal reserve is not in the recovered body (the body of the other) for the reason that it remains deeply invested at the level of the body proper, what is called auto-erotism. What is the point of introducing an "autism" of jouissance here? It is to clearly emphasize that the drive is not shareable as such, neither at the imaginary level nor at the symbolic level, and that the erogenous rim (lips, sexual organs) constitutes the demarcation line between what is "deeply invested" of the body proper, this remainder, and the image, or the signifier. It goes without saying that these remarks on autism indicate its exact opposite, because the description he has just given us is anything but autistic.

Notes

1 Lacan J., "The function and field of speech and language in psychoanalysis", in *Ecrits*, W. W. Norton & Company, 2006, p. 262.
2 "Everything happens as if, as soon as it's a question of an unconscious desire, we find ourselves in the presence of a mecha- nism, a necessary *Spaltung* which makes desire— which for a long time we have presumed alienated in a quite special relationship with the other—appear here as marked, not only by the need for an intermediary in the other as such, but also by the mark of a special signifier, a chosen signifier, which here happens to be the obligatory path which, as it were, the course of the vital force, desire in this case, must follow.", Lacan J., *Formations of the Unconscious: The Seminar of Jacques Lacan*, Polity Press, 2020, p. 309.
3 Brooks R. and Meltzoff A., "The importance of eyes: How infants interpret adult looking behavior", *Developmental Psychology*, 38(6), 2002, p. 958–966.
4 Lacan J., *The Object Relation, The Seminar of Jacques Lacan, Book IV*, translated by A. R. Price, Polity, 2020, p. 39.
5 Lacan J., *Formations of the Unconscious: The Seminar of Jacques Lacan*, Polity Press, 2020, p. 372.
6 Lévi-Strauss C., *Introduction to the Work of Marcel Mauss*, Routledge and Kegan Paul, London, 1987, p. 21.
7 "Any society at all is therefore comparable to a universe in which only discrete masses are highly structured. So, in any society, it would be inevitable that a percentage (itself variable) of individuals find themselves placed 'off system', so to speak, or between two or more irreducible systems. The group seeks and even requires of those individuals that they figuratively represent certain forms of compromise which are not realisable on the collective plane; that they simulate imaginary transitions, embody incompatible syntheses. ", Lévi-Strauss C., *Introduction to the Work of Marcel Mauss*, Routledge and Kegan Paul, London, 1987, p. 18.
8 Lévi-Strauss C., *Introduction to the Work of Marcel Mauss*, Routledge and Kegan Paul, London, 1987, p. 54.
9 Hénaff M., *Claude Lévi-Strauss et l'anthropologie structurale*, éd. Pierre Belfond, Paris, 1991, p. 343. Freud S., "The uncanny", in S. Freud (Ed.), *The Standard Edition of the Complete Psychological Works of Sigmund Freud, Volume XVII (1917–1919)*, London the Hogarth Press, 1966.
10 Mauss M. and Hubert H., *Esquisse d'une théorie générale de la magie*, présentation de F. Keck et A. Morvan, PUF, Quadrige, Paris, 2019.
11 Freud S., "The uncanny", in *The Revised Standard Edition of the Complete Psychological Works of Sigmund Freud*, translated by James Strachey and Mark Solms, Volume XVII, Revised edition, Rowman & Littlefield, London, 2024.
12 Jentsch E., *Zur Psychologie Des Unheimlichen*, Kessinger Publishing, 2010; Jentsch E., "On the psychology of the uncanny (1906)", *Angelaki, Journal of the Theoretical Humanities*, 2(1), 1997. http://dx.doi.org/10.1080/09697259708571910

13 Freud S., "The uncanny", in *The Revised Standard Edition of the Complete Psychological Works of Sigmund Freud*, Volume XVII, Revised edition, translated by James Strachey and Mark Solms, Rowman & Littlefield, London, 2024.
14 Mori M., "The uncanny valley", *IEEE Robotics & Automation Magazine*, *19*, 2012, p. 98–100.
15 Descola P., *Par-delà nature et culture*, Gallimard, Paris, 2005.
16 Regarding a critique of Lévi-Strauss's reading of Mauss, see also Rochat P., *Others in Mind: Social Origins of Self-Consciousness*, Cambridge University Press, Cambridge, 2009.
17 "Looking at the development of neonates, it appear that the fear of separation and rejection is a *consequence* of attachement rather than a cause", Rochat P., *Others in Mind: Social Origins of Self-Consciousness*, Cambridge University Press, Cambridge, 2009, p. 25.
18 Lacan J., *Anxiety: The Seminar of Jacques Lacan, Book X*, Polity Press, Malden, 2014, p. 26–27.
19 Lacan J., *The Four Fundamental Concepts of Psycho-Analysis*, Routledge, 2004, p. 68.
20 "An opaque construction is one in which you cannot in general supplant a singular term by a *codesignative* term (one referring to the same object) without disturbing the truth value of the containing sentence". Quine W. V. O., *Word and Object*, The M.I.T. Press, 1960, p. 151.
21 "Human symbolic systems are uniquely creative and deliberate in fostering shared meanings about things, especially about the self. No other animals dwell on and cultivate pretense, deception, or simulation for main purpose of moving, controlling, and eventually seducing the mind of others", Rochat P., *Others in Mind: Social Origins of Self-Consciousness*, Cambridge University Press, Cambridge, 2009, p. 19.
22 "Now, there is no more anxiety if orgasm comes to cover it back over". Lacan J., *Anxiety: The Seminar of Jacques Lacan, Book X*, Polity Press, Malden, 2014, p. 262.
23 "The family complexes", translated by Carolyn Asp in *Critical Texts*, *5*(3), 1988. Also translated by Andrea Kahn in *Semiotext 10*, *4*(1), 1981. In *Autres Écrits*, Seuil, Paris, 2001.
24 Lacan J., *The Four Fundamental Concepts of Psycho-Analysis*, Routledge, 2004, p. 199.
25 Miller J.-A., "L'objet jouissance", *Revue La cause du désir, L'objet caché*, *94*, November 2016, p. 102.
26 Rochat P., "Five levels of self-awareness as they unfold early in life", *Consciousness and Cognition, 12*, 2003, p. 717–731.
27 Lacan J., "The mirror stage as formative of the I function", in *Ecrits*, W. W. Norton & Company, 2006, p. 77.
28 Lacan J., "The mirror stage as formative of the I function", in *Ecrits*, W. W. Norton & Company, 2006, p. 77.
29 Lacan J., "The subversion of the subject and the dialectic of desire", in *Ecrits*, W. W. Norton & Company, 2006, p. 688.
30 Bruner J., *Child's Talk, Learning to Use Language*, W. W. Norton & Co, New York, 1983.
31 Baron-Cohen S., *Mindblindness: An Essay on Autism and Theory of Mind*, The MIT Press, Boston, 1995, p. 108.
32 Russell's paradox can be stated as follows: Does the set of all sets that do not contain themselves contain itself? If one answers yes, then by definition, the members of this set do not contain themselves, so it does not contain itself: contradiction. But if one answers no, then it has the required property of containing itself: contradiction again.
33 Lacan J., *Anxiety: The Seminar of Jacques Lacan, Book X*, Polity Press, Malden, 2014, p. 91.
34 Winnicott D. W., *Playing and Reality*, Taylor & Francis Group, New York, 1991.

35 "Yes, the 'little a' is a concept I invented to designate the object of desire. The 'little a' is what Winnicott calls the transitional object . . . I had the chance to meet Winnicott." Lacan was able to assert this on February 2, 1975, at The French Institute in London. http://ecole-lacanienne.net/wp-content/uploads/2016/04/1975-02-03.pdf.

36 Lacan J., "Allocutions sur les psychoses chez l'enfant", in *Autres Ecrits*, Seuil, Paris, 2001, p. 368.

37 Lacan J., "Allocutions sur les psychoses chez l'enfant", in *Autres Ecrits*, Seuil, Paris, 2001, p. 368.

38 Winnicott D. W., *Playing and Reality*, Taylor & Francis Group, New York, 1991.

39 Winnicott D. W., *Playing and Reality*, Taylor & Francis Group, New York, 1991.

40 Winnicott D. W., *Playing and Reality*, Taylor & Francis Group, New York, 1991.

41 "The transitional object, which Lacan initially situates in the imaginary register, cannot be reduced to something simply imaginary because it is a tertiary object, existing between the mother and the child and objecting to the dual relationship", Vanier A., "Winnicott and Lacan: A missed encounter", *The Psychoanalytic Quarterly, LXXXI*(2), 2012, p. 284–285.

42 Lacan J., *Anxiety: The Seminar of Jacques Lacan, Book X*, Polity Press, Malden, 2014, p. 44.

43 Lacan J., *Anxiety: The Seminar of Jacques Lacan, Book X*, Polity Press, Malden, 2014, p. 44.

44 Let us note that the same diagram had already been used in the seminar *L'identification* (unpublished) in the November 15, 1961 session.

45 Lacan J., *Anxiety: The Seminar of Jacques Lacan, Book X*, Polity Press, Malden, 2014, p. 44–45.

46 Lacan J., *The Four Fundamental Concepts of Psycho-Analysis*, Routledge, 2004, p. 62.

47 Lacan J., *Anxiety: The Seminar of Jacques Lacan, Book X*, Polity Press, Malden, 2014, p. 44–45.

48 Lacan J., *Anxiety: The Seminar of Jacques Lacan, Book X*, Polity Press, Malden, 2014, p. 44.

49 Lacan J., *Anxiety: The Seminar of Jacques Lacan, Book X*, Polity Press, Malden, 2014, p. 40.

50 Lacan J., *The Four Fundamental Concepts of Psycho-Analysis*, Routledge, 2004, p. 194.

51 Agamben G., *Profanations*, Zone Books, New York, 2007, p. 12.

52 "To deny a statement is to affirm another statement", in W. V. O. Quine (Ed.), *Methods of Logic*, Fourth edition, Harvard University Press, Cambridge, MA, 1982, p. 9.

53 Agamben G., *Profanations*, Zone Books, New York, 2007, p. 14.

54 Agamben G., *Profanations*, Zone Books, New York, 2007, p. 18.

55 Lacan J., *Anxiety: The Seminar of Jacques Lacan, Book X*, Polity Press, Malden, 2014, p. 45.

56 Lacan J., *Anxiety: The Seminar of Jacques Lacan, Book X*, Polity Press, Malden, 2014, p. 45.

Chapter 3

Kant's Transcendental Aesthetic, and Ours

Kant begins his *Critique of Pure Reason* with a kind of Copernican revolution in the problem of knowledge: in the first part devoted to transcendental aesthetics, which deals with the conditions of the possibility of knowing objects in the sensible world, he develops the idea that space and time are the two a priori conditions of perception. To use his own words, "Space is not an empirical concept that has been drawn from outer experiences.[1]" In other words, everything related to perception (vision, for example) assumes space as an a priori form in which sensible matter is inscribed.

Thus, for Kant, space is an a priori, transcendental intuition, independent of experience. For Kant, time and space do not exist in themselves in the sense that they are objective realities; they are inherent in the perceiver, and they do not derive from experience but condition it. This is why they are called a priori. For Kant, space is thus an a priori form of sensibility. In this sense, there is no perception that is not spatial; objects, as they are given in sensible experience, are necessarily perceived as situated in space, and this space is not objective but subjective in that it is an a priori, a condition of the possibility of perception and representation.

Lacan considers this a priori conception of space the result of a *petitio principii* that would be part of the famous "function of misrecognition" that he attributes to the ego in his seminar on the ego, and even as early as his work on the mirror stage. One can only assume that there is a space that is just waiting to be filled with objects on the condition of presupposing (postulating) a consciousness that has to have been there forever to perceive the objects that populate this space.

Lacan's objection, which in particular concerns Kant's first critique, is centered on a critique of perception; he can thereby argue that this body is not taken over by the "pure and simple categories of transcendental.[2]" Perception can perceive everything that it is possible to perceive, except for the very apparatuses of perception. These apparatuses are part of this space that Kant considers as a priori. Thus, the body itself is part of this space, and with it, the organ of vision—namely, the eye—is part of this body and this a priori, unconditioned space. The body as organism and organ—and more precisely, the body as a border—is part of the space that makes perception possible.

DOI: 10.4324/9781003614203-3

In other words, it is as if Kant considered the body itself to be unquestionable and to be part of the a priori necessary for producing a pure aesthetic. This amounts to saying that he misrecognizes what matters most in perception—namely, the bodily border (the eye, for example). On the other hand, Lacan's critical idea is that the eye itself is both a means of and an obstacle to perception. Within the synthetic a priori course of perception that Kant would assume to be crystal clear, the eye could be, rather, an accident. Even better: the eye can see everything except itself.

This Kantian function of misrecognition results, notably, from a misrecognition of the body, which is why Lacan will say of this body, "nor is it given to us in a pure and simple way in the mirror.[3]" It is clear that for Lacan, neither space nor the body—which is part of this space—are concepts that go without saying, as Kant demands they be. They are not, as he claims, products of our intuition, and if we want to be even more precise, especially regarding this aspect of sensation (*aesthesis*; it is known that Kant used the word "aesthetic" in the pre-Baumgarten sense), which is vision, we might say that its body—the body of vision, the eye—is also not a product of direct intuition. There is no transparency regarding the eye. Contrary to the Lacanian position we are trying to grasp, Kant starts from the premise that space (the body, the eye) is a representation that is posited as a nonempirical "foundation" that makes "syntheses" (vision and what there is to see) possible.

Indeed, Kant writes,

> What then must the representation of space be for such a cognition of it to be possible? It must originally be intuition; for from a mere concept no propositions can be drawn that go beyond the concept, which, however, happens in geometry. But this intuition must be encountered in us a priori, i.e., prior to all perception of an object, thus it must be pure, not empirical intuition.[4]

What does this mean, if not that space as such, and with it the body that is part of it, is the product of an a priori intuition "before all perception of the object"? Lacan's objection to this Kantian position is the implication that this exclusion, this *petitio principii* that wants to create a sort of "Other of the Other" (if I may evoke this Lacanian notion of an Other that guarantees all perception, and thus, space) becomes the very condition of perception. Moreover, this guarantee of perception comes precisely from the Other (the concave mirror of the inverted bouquet experiment). Let us note this wonderful statement from Kant on cause: "the unconditioned necessity, which we need as the ultimate support of all things, is the true abyss of human reason." And here is Lacan, locating "the support of all things" and the cause of desire in the same place:

> Even Kant, Kant especially, I will say, remains steeped in causality, remains suspended from the justification . . . of this function, which is essential to the whole mechanism of the lived experience of our mental life, the function of cause. Across the board, the cause proves to be irrefutable, irreducible and almost ungraspable to critique. . . . This formalism doesn't only summon us and

furnish us with the frameworks of our thinking and our transcendental aesthetic, it seizes hold of us at a particular place. We give it not only the matter, not only our Being of thought, but the corporeal morsel that it torn from us as such. . . . This bodily portion of ourselves is, essentially and functionally, partial.[5]

Lacan therefore supposes that Kant's formulation of space as intuition—as the immediate apprehension of consciousness—overlooks the fact that any perception of an object, any desire related to an object, any objectality "is the corollary of a pathos of cutting.[6]" One must exclude a part of one's own flesh (the $(-\varphi)$ I have mentioned) so that there can be access to the flesh, to the object.

Let me be clear: in this sentence, the word "flesh" has two different meanings. The first "piece of flesh" remains a foreign body to the signifying machine mentioned above, while the second concept of flesh defines it as part of the signifying machine, or of the body—i(a)—as something that is not given to us in a pure and simple way. The eye is this part of space that would be almost "transparent," because it does not see itself, but which, because of this, is torn away from the living being; it must not see itself $(-\varphi)$ in order to be able to see i(a).

Thus, according to Lacan, vision and what one seeks to perceive through it are caused by this transparency of the body that we call "border," which is nothing other than an opening to the objects of desire. Just as Freud imagines a mouth that would kiss itself if it could, Lacan conceives of an eye that would like to see itself and that, failing to do so, contents itself with gazing at objects. This is why the object is a "pathos of cutting" and why, as Lacan indicates, the object a necessarily implies $(-\varphi)$, that is, a deprivation. In this sense, one might consider that according to Kantian doctrine, perception "is a perception without organs: it is reason that perceives and not the body.[7]"

At the risk of repeating myself, I will distinguish these two aspects of our transcendental aesthetics (Lacan's, which goes against Kant's): on the one hand, the signifier and on the other, a piece of flesh that is heterogeneous, even inadequate to it. Indeed, on the one hand, we know that "this formalism does not only require us and give us the frameworks of our thought and our transcendental aesthetics, it seizes us by some part," meaning that this formalism (these laws of the signifier) mutilates some part of the body (the eye, for example, and with it any other part that functions as a border). On the other hand, there is "this part of ourselves, this part of our flesh, that remains necessarily caught in the formal machine." Although it remains caught within it, this part is not treatable by the signifying machine; on the contrary, because it is by definition untreatable ("It is this part of ourselves that is caught in the machine, and which is forever irrecoverable"), it thereby becomes the cause of desire.

Kant is thus convenient, but we can only use him "to reconstitute for ourselves the transcendental aesthetics that fits our experience.[8]" Why? Because Lacan intends to reconstitute a critique of pure desire through his object a: "this pivotal locus of the pure function of desire, so to speak, this locus is the one in which I want to demonstrate for you how the a takes shape—a, the object of objects.[9]" We can deduce two consequences concerning the object a after reading this paragraph: 1) it is a place, just like space and just like the body; 2) this place has never been identified before Lacan, and it is the very condition of all desire. Just like Kant's a priori, this place establishes the object a as the a priori condition of any possible relationship to objects of desire. Lacan thus reconstructs Kant's transcendental critique, except that its place now seems to be the body and, in particular, what withdraws and separates from the body, a move that necessitates establishing a cut in the body, or a "pathos of cutting" alongside the object of desire. This place is (-φ). At each edge, at each cut, a particular pathos appears in the form of an object (gaze, feces, voice).

Why, then, would a transcendental aesthetics specific to psychoanalysis, specific to Lacan, and to understanding the object a, be necessary? Why, in other words, would a Lacanian transcendental aesthetics be necessary? Lacan explains, "I will say that objectality is the correlate to a pathos of the cut . . . this part of ourselves, this part of our flesh, which necessarily remains caught in the formal machine.[10]" This formulation—if I may put it this way—means that the flesh taken by the Other is definitively lost to the speaking being by way of the "turning of the head" that Lacan insists upon in his seminar on anxiety. It should be understood that if this part is forever irrecoverable, it is because the subject is turned away from the spec- ular image and, more precisely, because something in the image—something that the Other will ultimately come to pacify—fails to support the subject's distress, its already cut and fragmented flesh. The Other that the living being turns toward (and not only the imaginary other toward whom the child turns their head) represents a shift to another register and yet—if I dare say—leaves in the mirror's path this remainder that cannot be symbolized as such by the signifying machine.

For convenience, we can temporarily reduce the unsymbolizable remainder— which concerns the mirror and vision—to the gaze, and more precisely, to what in the gaze resists vision's knowledge. But in order that, after this head rotation, the subject be able to see, imagine, and relate to the other through the intermediary of fantasy, they will have no other choice but to rely on their mutilated flesh on the condition of acting as if it were not mutilated, as if it were not missing.

Finally, I suppose that we must understand the pathos of cutting in the Kantian sense of the term, namely as a sensible, phenomenological, and *a posteriori* expe- rience, which is quite different from the cut as a "pure" form—that is, the body constructed by holes and edges. Thus, Kant can speak of a "pathological love" that is very different from "practical" love, the latter being at the basis of love as will, or as goodwill. We can even assume that in both his construction of the object a and his critique of transcendental aesthetics, Lacan emphasizes the cut rather than the pathos—rather than the object—even if it is indeed the object a that is at stake.[11]

The Experience of the Double and the Object a: "Lack Comes to Lack"

There is a considerable amount of literature on the figure of the double both in psychoanalysis and in the world of fiction. One only needs to think of Dostoevsky's novel *The Double* and the story "Le Horla," not to mention Otto Rank's essay on the subject, as well as the experience of the specular double and the anxiety it arouses described by Freud in his text *The Uncanny*. It is likely that Kant did not have at his disposal the elements specific to a psychology of experience—and even less so those of experimental psychology—to deal with the double, but it is a subject that might have interested him; the image of one's own body—a sensible experience, a phenomenon and not a noumenon—assails the understanding.

Sensibility is prepared a priori to perceive the image of one's own body at a given moment (time) and in a specific place (space). But if the experience of the double is worthy of its name, it is because something comes to disorient the perceiver—something that seems out of sync in both time and space relative to an understanding configured a priori; this something is generally an image, in particular one's own image but as seen by another. Thus, one experiences how the body is not just a perceptive entity that occupies space.

This misrecognition is nevertheless established in the living being from the moment that it must look elsewhere than its own image, since it must look toward a third party. The image of one's own body can only be perceived through the vision of the other; the mirror itself functions as a perceiving eye, an eye that the subject's eye naturally does not see. And it is because this eye must especially remain hidden that this image of ourselves—which is captured from the outside—can possibly acquire the status of the gaze.

Why is fixing one's own gaze in the mirror unsettling or disturbing (an experience similar to that felt when hearing the echo of one's own voice on the telephone)? Because it makes present the fact that it is not vision that is at play in the apprehension of the world but rather what makes a stain within the very process of vision. Not only can the image acquire the status of the gaze, but this gaze is implied by definition from the moment we suppose another who objectifies us. In other words, we find in the image something other than this image—namely, this possible eye of the other that we can begin to call "gaze" for the simple reason that it is no longer the apparatus of perception itself. We thus find something else that, at times, slightly exceeds the mere image, the only image that we perceive.

If these indications are pertinent, then we have two distinct modalities of the manifestation of this other thing through the experience of the double: either the image is not what it should be in time and space, or it is the identical reflection of the object but in a time and/or space that is inadequate with the a priori of understanding, and therefore that of the perceiver. Thus, we find a theme dear to Lacan and pertinent to the conception of the object a: the split between the gaze and vision. To put it another way: the experience of the double is that of the subject and not that of the self; it is that of the real and not that of reality.

In light of the text by Wallon that I mentioned earlier, it is not surprising that the specular double manifests itself in different ways in clinical psychopathology, not to mention the variations of related phenomena that we can frequently observe in normal individuals. But pathology should draw our attention, if we consider that the prevalence of imaginary phenomena is very strong in psychotics. For example, Lacan seems categorical when he indicates, in his seminar on *Anxiety*, that if the head rotation—that is, the possibility of detaching from the narcissistic image—does not take place, then there is no repression. He was also categorical in his seminar *Psychoses*:

> Let's suppose that this situation entails for the subject the impossibility of assuming the realization of the signifier *father* at the symbolic level. What'she left with? He's left with the image the paternal function is reduced to. It's an image which isn't inscribed in any triangular dialectic.[12]

Lacan goes on to clarify, however, an important clinical distinction between the prevalence of imaginary phenomena and the imaginary capture specific to psychosis:

> If the captivating image is without limits, if the character in question manifests himself simply in the order of strength and not in that of the pact, then a relation of rivalry, aggressiveness, fear, etc. appear. Insofar as the relationship remains on the imaginary, dual, and unlimited plane, it doesn't possess the meaning of reciprocal exclusion that is included in specular confrontation, but possesses instead the other function, that of imaginary capture. . . . The alienation here is radical, it isn't bound to a nihilating signified, as in a certain type of rivalrous relation with the father, but to a nihilation of the signifier.[13]

It is as if the whole of the signifying order is at stake and, with it, this particular signifier that has not allowed for a distance to be established—through a signifying annihilation—from one's specular image (in other words, from the specular image of the other).

For a good Kantian, dealing with one's own body is not far from an oxymoron. The image is the phenomenon; one's own body would be what most resembles a thing in itself, or a noumenon. The image of one's own body would be an example of a synthetic a priori judgment, which would validate Kant if the experience of the double, along with other imaginary and bodily phenomena, did not in fact challenge the Kantian critique of perception. For what is even more radical than Kant's theory is the fact that these experiences are present in every speaking being, so that we do not have to evoke the schizophrenic's transitivism, echopraxia, or thought echo to evoke the notion of the double. This presence can, at any moment and in various forms, manifest in those beings subjected to repression. What do I mean by this? Why evoke echopraxia or thought echo? For a simple reason: it is surprising that when dealing with the gaze and the voice as objects, one readily cites the examples of the mirror and the tape recorder—or simply the telephone—to the extent that these latter technical devices can derealize perception and disturb it.

In *Anxiety*, Lacan studies this dimension of the double through the notion of the uncanny, or *Unheimlichkeit*. I have already explained, in my reading of Lacan, that (-φ) is precisely what escapes the specular image. To put it differently: in the place of (-φ), one sees nothing other than the object of desire. If one were to see something other than what is supposed to be seen, we could say that they would be confronted with the presence of a presence. We need only quote the following passage where, after having just drawn the inverted bouquet diagram on the board, Lacan explains, "I've written (-φ) at the top, because we'll have to put it there next time. This minus-*phi* is no more visible, no more tangible, no more presentifiable up there than down here, under i(a), because it hasn't entered the imaginary.[14]"

In other words, (-φ) corresponds to all that is nonspecularizable (and nonaudible), to all that is not supposed to appear in the reflected or perceived image (the image of one's own body or the image of the other). One's own body necessarily contains something that cannot be captured by the image; the three-dimensionality of the body escapes the two-dimensionality of the image. Even looking at oneself with more than one mirror risks being surprised by partial images that we are not used to seeing (and that, indeed, we may have never seen). In short, we inhabit the world of the image but with the instruments of language, those that do not belong to the imaginary.

Agamben, recalling Hamann's objection to Kant, says,

> This is where full weight must be given to Hamann's critique of Kant, which renders meaningless any idea of pure reason 'elevated as a transcendental subject' and asserted as independent of language; for 'not only does the faculty of thought wholly reside in language, but language is also reason's central misunderstanding of itself'.[15]

The consequence of the primacy of language (the symbolic) is a "nonimaginarizable" register that produces a double effect: on the one hand, it allows us to grasp the image without being burdened by what de-completes this image, that is, without being haunted by the blind spot of the rearview mirror; but on the other hand, what escapes the image creates a sort of traumatic focal point, a sudden appearance that undermines the totality of the image to which we are accustomed. This focal point is that of anxiety.

I would like to conclude by commenting on this passage and more precisely on the expression "there is no image of the lack," for it could give rise to misunderstandings. And just as the witticism appears where it might not appear (let us say the same of a slip of the tongue, which could in turn reveal itself to be anxiety-inducing), so too does the Unheimlich bring forth anxiety. To put it another way: (-φ) is your image in the mirror as you see it every day; there is no image of the lack, and everything happens as expected. But when something about your image troubles you (let us recall our hero Freud on the train), it is this usual lack (-φ) that is missing, leading to anxiety. I suggest retaining this way of understanding Lacan's oft-repeated adage (anxiety arises when the lack lacks) in order to avoid clouding our minds.

After all, isn't this the same Lacan who complains about understanding too quickly what the uncanny is? I thus allow myself—hoping that I won't tire my reader with this series of quotations that seem, however, necessary to me—to evoke in full Lacan's words intended to define anxiety as an affect, or as an experience that is supposed to escape the entire signifying structure:

> Anxiety, I've told you, is linked to anything that might appear at the place (-φ). What assures us of this is a phenomenon for which the too scant attention that's been paid to it has meant that nobody has arrived at a formulation that would be satisfactory and unified for the functions of anxiety in their entirety in the field of our experience. of all the functions of anxiety in the field of our experience. This phenomenon is the *Unheimliche*.[16]

Here is a first question: why do we need a phenomenon that assures us of this place of anxiety? With the use of such a signifier, it is almost as if Lacan is thinking of Kant. In other words, why must strangeness be of the order of the phenomenon? Why does it belong to the realm of the phenomenon, and moreover, of a single phenomenon? And again, why does Lacan resort to this sort of "presence"—that is, a positivity—to account for an experience that is rather exceptional, which is that of anxiety? With the experience of the double and other related phenomena, we are clearly faced with manifestations of the object a as positivity, and not only in a negative, symbolic conception of the lack of the object.

The first answer to our previous question is to suggest that anxiety is not exceptional and that it underlies all relationships to desire; anxiety as a phenomenon only indicates what it translates from the noumenon, the object a, or "object of objects." The second thing we might recall is that Lacan had promised, a few pages earlier, a "presence"—that of an object (the noumenon) and not only the theory of a lost object, or a lack of object. Let us note in passing that Freud's lost object is not an object; what is an object is what is found in its place—namely, the narcissistic object of desire, or the rediscovered object.

This last remark also applies to Lacan's object a, which cannot be an object of desire. But there is a difference between Freud's negative (the lost object) and Lacan's positive (the object a), which is that the former can remain at the stage of a mere hypothesis without the Freudian edifice being jeopardized. For how can one demonstrate the presence of something that is supposed to be, by definition, absent? One can be content with its absence. In the case of Lacan's object a, however, it is more difficult to avoid attempting to show it since, according to Lacan, it implies a presence. Anxiety is not without object, he tells us; it does not exist without the shadow of a presence. Very well, but what kind of presence is it? Lacan says this just before mentioning the idea that anxiety is linked "to everything that can appear in the place (-φ) (in other words, where nothing should appear). Except that something can appear, and this is Lacan's demonstration. How does he manage to make this 'appearance' felt where Freud is content with the notion of a lost object? Well, he is forced to take a step back.

Indeed, Lacan cannot address the phenomenon of the *Unheimlichkeit* without taking a "step back", where one believed that he had taken a step forward by placing the (-φ) outside the visible image, i(a). I'll quote the words Lacan uses when addressing what is called castration anxiety: "I might has been faster with my disquisition this morning that I intended [in my opinion, "the step forward"]. Either way, you can see here an indication that there might be a possible way through ["*il y a peut-être la possibilité de passage*"].[17]

Thus, it becomes clear that if there is a possibility to make absence present, it exists only through the imaginary register ("imaginary castration . . . in its full right"), which implies a certain "going back." We can suppose that the word "passage" articulates two movements: progression and regression. They function here as follows: everything that moves from the imaginary to the symbolic is progressive, necessarily implying a supremacy of the symbolic over the imaginary, which is thereby displaced or relativized; everything that, once installed in the symbolic, returns to the continuity of the imaginary, that is, the register where objects and images are reversible and where anxiety is generally avoided, is regressive. The child who turns his head away from the mirror toward something else, toward the object whose image is reflected in the mirror, progresses. The child who, having discovered this other dimension, smiles as he returns to the image reflected in the mirror, regresses somewhat, thereby avoiding the potential anxiety linked to the doubling of the image (Wallon), or to the annihilation of the image by the signifier, to refer to Lacan's statement in *Psychoses*.

Unheimlichkeit

In other words, Lacan took a long detour in order to introduce the notion of lack: (-φ), which we must understand as that which is not visible in the mirror and must use to convey the nonspecularizable dimension of the object, a dimension that corresponds to the drive as autistic and nonshareable. He then, through a backward passage, demonstrated the impact of this nonspecularizable, nonshareable aspect on the unsettling and anxiety-inducing imaginary; this passage occurs through the "castration complex," which allows for "the study of the phenomenology of anxiety." This imaginary—the phenomenon of the *Unheimlichkeit*—is unsettling, but it remains specularizable, potentially shareable, and, all things considered, not very autistic.

What is *Unheimlichkeit*? We know that Freud emphasized the kinship between the familiar (*Heim*) and the unfamiliar (*Unheim*), the latter becoming unsettling primarily because of its familiarity. The familiar and the unsettling can easily be reversible. What is the familiar? It is (-φ). Lacan states this explicitly. Lacan also calls this (-φ), or this *Heim*, "the house of man." In other words, it is the symbolic world, the one constructed by the signifier, a topic I addressed in my first chapter. It is therefore clear that there is an absence produced by the structure and that this void created by the Other (the producer of absence) can manifest as what it is— namely, a positivity. Lacan rejects Hegel, but only by validating him; if the word is the murder of the thing, this murder cannot occur once and for all without the risk of the return of a revenant, or a specter of the murdered thing: the uncanny.

Except that this return will only occur through a backward step, the perfect reverse of the "step forward" of the structure, or of the installation of the symbolic world—even of the gesture of the child turning his head described by Wallon. If the step forward produces (-φ), (*Heim*, or the introduction of the living being into the symbolic world), the backward step (this possibility can only be explored by going back to the place where imaginary castration operates) is nothing but its reverse—namely, a presence—*Unheim*—or what is called the object a, a presence that must by definition remain non-specularizable and that is not visible as such. Except that through the experience of the double, this presence shows its tip, the tip that Lacan calls a "step without an object."

W.W.

To conclude, I cite an example of this positivity as it is presented in the experience of the double in the short story by Edgar Allan Poe titled "William Wilson[18]" and brilliantly commented on by Otto Rank. The argument is known: a man named William Wilson, whose initials are W.W.—thus evoking the "double U"—has, in his childhood, a strange encounter. At his school, there is an almost perfect double who bears his same first and last name and who resembles him so closely that they are like two peas in a pod. He is troubled by this strangeness, and the story insists on the fact that there is no kinship between them. Poe writes,

His cue, which was to perfect an imitation of myself, lay both in words and in actions; and most admirably did he play his part. My dress it was an easy matter to copy; my gait and general manner were, without difficulty, appropriated; in spite of his constitutional defect, even my voice did not escape him. My louder tones were, of course, unattempted, but then the key, it was identical; and his singular whisper, it grew the very echo of my own.

Yet the character realizes that he is the only one who notices this imitation and, therefore, the only one to experience this sort of doubling:

I had but one consolation—in the fact that the imitation, apparently, was noticed by myself alone, and that I had to endure only the knowing and strangely sarcastic smiles of my namesake himself.

Very well, but is that all? Certainly not. There is a detail that makes this already quite unsettling double show its double strangeness—a strangeness within a strangeness, or a detail that escapes the mere copy-paste effect:

I could find, indeed, but one vulnerable point, and that, lying in a personal peculiarity, arising, perhaps, from constitutional disease, would have been spared by any antagonist less at his wit's end than myself;—my rival had a weakness in the faucal or guttural organs, which precluded him from raising his voice at any time above a very low whisper.

We thus notice that in the register of objects that detach themselves from the copy, there is not only the gaze, as I suggested, but also other "positive objects" or ruses that are cuts into the purely imaginary register. In this case, we have the voice—not only the voice in its sonic materiality but something in the voice that lets us hear something other than what this voice says, "in spite of his constitutional defect, even my voice did not escape him. My louder tones were, of course, unattempted, but then the key, it was identical; and his singular whisper, it grew the very echo of my own."

It is the echo of the voice, or the duplication that is not one, that opens the disparity between the two figures. In this case, this disparity serves the living being to reassure themselves regarding the force of imaginary capture: "my rival had a weakness in the faucal or guttural organs, which precluded him from raising his voice at any time above a very low whisper. Of this defect I did not fall to take what poor advantage lay in my power."

The theme of the voice returns in the text, notably when the double reappears after several years of calm:

"Gentlemen," he said, in a low, distinct, and never-to-be-forgotten whisper which thrilled to the very marrow of my bones, "Gentlemen, I make no apology for this behaviour, because in thus behaving, I am but fulfilling a duty. You are, beyond doubt, uninformed of the true character of the person who has to-night won at ecarte a large sum of money from Lord Glendinning. I will therefore put you upon an expeditious and decisive plan of obtaining this very necessary information. Please to examine, at your leisure, the inner linings of the cuff of his left sleeve, and the several little packages which may be found in the somewhat capacious pockets of his embroidered morning wrapper." While he spoke, so profound was the stillness that one might have heard a pin drop upon the floor.

The double allows the character to stop a manic escalation when he wins at the game. Sometimes the voice takes control over him, and sometimes it is he—our hero—who takes control over the other: "– Wretch!—I cried in a voice hoarse with rage, and every syllable that escaped me was like fuel for the fire of my anger." The story ends with a duel between the character and his double—a face-to-face in which he kills his double, at which point there is a surprising head turn, almost as if Poe had read Wallon and Lacan:

In a few seconds I forced him by sheer strength against the wainscoting, and thus, getting him at mercy, plunged my sword, with brute ferocity, repeatedly through and through his bosom. At that instant some person tried the latch of the door. I hastened to prevent an intrusion, and then immediately returned to my dying antagonist. But what human language can adequately portray that astonishment, that horror which possessed me at the spectacle then presented to view? The brief moment in which I averted my eyes had been sufficient to produce, apparently, a material change in the arrangements at the upper or farther end of the room. A large mirror,—so at first it seemed to me in my confusion—now stood where none had been perceptible before; and, as I stepped up to it in extremity of terror, mine own image, but with features all pale and dabbled in blood, advanced to meet me with a feeble and tottering gait.

The turning of the head is enough to change the scenery and put things back into place; the act of killing the other is enough to reintroduce, albeit a bit too late, the symbolic dimension that had been absent since the character entered the school and believed he had supremacy over the other imaginary figures, over the multiplicity of speaking beings with which he was confronted.

To conclude this long chapter, we can discern in the path I have taken here the importance that Lacan placed on the possibility of something strange emerging in any image, insofar as it is constituted by another strangeness, what psychoanalysis calls libido. If one thinks that the erogenous rims ('autistic') imply an object (partner) that would come to satisfy them, this partner is inevitably contaminated by the autistic erogenous rims. But with this description, we are in the Freudian realm, that of repetition and of the rediscovery of the 'lost' object. Lacan would add the following: since the other is naturally an other, just as the gaze of the other is in its face, it is in this sense that the other contains the probable emergence of the unpredictable or the unexpected, of what risks slipping away from us. And this is what orients our unconscious desire (and not just a 'desire for' the object). In the same way that our body is subsumed by the socialized other, the most intimate part of the body (the drive) is sequestered in the field of the other. This is why the drive can return to the body 'from the outside,' and thus from the place of extimacy—the ego ideal, depersonalization, and even psychosis—if we consider Lacan's idea that what erupts in madness comes from the outside, or from the other, proving that it is precisely the other that is rejected in delirium and hallucination.

Notes

1 Kant I., *Critique of Pure Reason*, Cambridge University Press, Cambridge, 1998, p. 157.
2 Lacan J., *Anxiety: The Seminar of Jacques Lacan, Book X*, Polity Press, Malden, 2014, p. 88.
3 Lacan J., *Anxiety: The Seminar of Jacques Lacan, Book X*, Polity Press, Malden, 2014, p. 88.
4 Kant I., *Critique of Pure Reason*, Cambridge University Press, Cambridge, 1998, p. 176.
5 Lacan J., *Anxiety: The Seminar of Jacques Lacan, Book X*, Polity Press, Malden, 2014, p. 215.
6 Lacan J., *Anxiety: The Seminar of Jacques Lacan, Book X*, Polity Press, Malden, 2014, p. 214.
7 I owe this idea to Jean-Claude Milner (personal communication).

8 Lacan J., *Anxiety: The Seminar of Jacques Lacan, Book X*, Polity Press, Malden, 2014, p. 88.
9 Lacan J., *Anxiety: The Seminar of Jacques Lacan, Book X*, Polity Press, Malden, 2014, p. 214.
10 Lacan J., *Anxiety: The Seminar of Jacques Lacan, Book X*, Polity Press, Malden, 2014, p. 214.
11 '"For a critique of the Kantian position, one can also refer to E. Mach", in *The Analysis of Sensations: The Relation of the Physical to the Psychical*, Ed. Jacqueline Chambon, Paris, 1988 (especially ch. 1). I thank J.-C. Milner for this reference.'
12 Lacan J., *The Psychoses 1955–1956. The Seminar of Jacques Lacan, Book 3*, W. W. Norton & Co Inc., New York, London, 1993, p. 204.
13 Lacan J., *The Psychoses 1955–1956. The Seminar of Jacques Lacan, Book 3*, W. W. Norton & Co Inc., New York, London, 1993, p. 205.
14 Lacan J., *Anxiety: The Seminar of Jacques Lacan, Book X*, Polity Press, Malden, 2014, p. 41.
15 Agamben G., *Infancy and History, Essays on the Destruction of Experience*, Verso, London, 1993, p. 44.
16 Lacan J., *Anxiety: The Seminar of Jacques Lacan, Book X*, Polity Press, Malden, 2014, p. 47.
17 Lacan J., *Anxiety: The Seminar of Jacques Lacan, Book X*, Polity Press, Malden, 2014, p. 46.
18 Poe E. A., *Collected Works of Edgar Allan Poe*, Volume 2, edited by Thomas Ollive Mabbott, Harvard University Press, Cambridge, 1969.

Chapter 4

What Is Called Fantasy in Psychoanalysis?

The word "fantasy" has, over time, acquired a kind of conceptual and referential opacity, to the point of becoming ambiguous. In Freud, the term seems to refer to a general mental activity, equivalent at times it is true to a sexual activity. This sexual activity is more or less sublimated but no less connected to libido, or the libidinal reserve.

In Freud's writings, and notably in his most famous work, *The Interpretation of Dreams*, the term fantasy is regularly linked to daydreaming, thus evoking a dream-like register. However, in daydreaming—unlike in dreaming—the dreamer is the creator or the maker of "dreams," whereas in a dream, he is merely a spectator or voyeur, as Lacan points out in one of his seminars. There is indeed a kind of paradigm shift here that itself could give meaning to what we are trying to grasp in this work. Indeed, one could argue—and this will be formulated many times in this book—that for psychoanalysis, the subject is reduced to an object. This means that even in conscious daydreaming, the dreamer is much more of an object than he supposes. In other words, there is a kind of inversion in the relationship of the living being to his images such that he is more alienated from them than he would be as either creator or simple observer.

This alienation from images is evident in the fact that the "dreamer" (the one who imagines stories, who daydreams) becomes entirely dependent on them. These conscious daydreams that populate his/her daily life and that he/she knows so well are even stronger than simple reality, if by reality we mean our daily life that we know by heart. This is the sort of daily life (isn't Freud also the author of *Psychopathology of Everyday Life*?) that flows naturally and would only present to the living being a few moments of awakening in which he/she would be confronted with something else, with an "other scene," as Freud would say.

At this point, it is necessary to affirm two things: on the one hand, daydreaming is reality itself in the sense that it is in continuity with the ego; on the other hand, daydreaming conditions reality much more than reality conditions daydreaming. It is as if reality were only there to bring about diurnal material, just like what happens in dreams. Let's take a simple, tiny, but exemplary sample, in the Freudian sense that "the example is the thing itself." A three-year-old child, Jules, is very excited by the noisy atmosphere of a children's party. The other

DOI: 10.4324/9781003614203-4

children, older than him, are dancing to the rhythm of the music that plays continuously, but Jules becomes very insistent in demanding a particular song; no one listens to him, and he becomes anxious. The adults intervene to satisfy him and play the much-requested music. The child's response is unexpected: instead of dancing like the others, he remains dreamy, frozen, smiling, probably imagining some situation, while the adults are surprised and ask Jules to dance, as it was assumed that this was what he wanted. This is a good example of the hold that daydreaming (perhaps he saw himself dancing to the rhythm of the song) has on reality—it conditions reality, even determining the dreamer's behavior (aren't we surprised to see a person walking alone in the street, lost in thought with a smile on their face?). But the question we must now ask is: do these fantasies, daydreams, and imagination that are in immediate continuity with reality exhaust what we mean by fantasy in psychoanalysis? Certainly not, and it can already be affirmed that in a sense, daydreaming is in itself a kind of denial of fantasy, a fantasy disconnected from reality but in a continuous relationship, this time, with the drive.

A Child Is Being Beaten

As everyone knows, the prototypical model of Freudian fantasy originates in the 1919 article "A Child is Being Beaten.[1]" It is also interesting to highlight the subtitle of the essay: "Contribution to the Knowledge of the Genesis of Sexual Perversions." Upon closer examination, however, Freud had already dealt with the question well before this, so much so that this clinical example—evoked by Freud as a "fantasy representation" admitted "with astonishing frequency"—is a kind of clinical accomplishment developed by the father of psychoanalysis.

Before continuing our commentary, let's be clear about how this "fantasy representation" presents itself: it involves masturbation during which the way to reach orgasm is to imagine the scene of a child being beaten. And although this masturbation is sought after by the person in question, it sometimes (often?) becomes a source of discomfort, so much so that the masturbatory activity cannot be stopped and becomes compulsive, even a source of shame and guilt. Of course, the admission of this fantasy is accompanied by a feeling of embarrassment and shame, as is the case with most sexual fantasies that accompany the act of masturbation.

For Freud, this type of fantasy—although recreated by the person in adolescence or adulthood—actually originates in childhood, probably "from the fifth and sixth year." One may wonder at Freud's precision regarding the age at which this image, this representation, begins—how can he be so certain? We will see that he draws this information from six clinical cases—two men and four women—followed by himself. The sample is small, yet he allows himself to assert that this type of fantasy is encountered with astonishing frequency and that it can be situated at a precise age. It is important to emphasize that the representation originates before school age, so that when the child sees real scenes of flogging at school, they only awaken in him what he already knew:

> The influence of the school was so clear that the patients concerned were at first tempted to trace back their beating phantasies exclusively to these impressions of school life, which dated from later than their sixth year. But it was never possible for them to maintain that position; the phantasies had already been in existence before.[2]

It is clear that the patient always (or almost always) brings the scene back to school, to his school experience—and yet Freud demonstrates that this is not the case ("that never held"). Let us clarify further, since the time in which Freud writes is not ours, that what is being described is the flogging of children by adults (punishments administered by teachers) and not by other children. This remark will make full sense later on in my commentary.

So far, we must content ourselves with a rather sparse structure of the fantasy in question. It is safe to say that Freud is not stingy with details—quite the contrary—and yet the narrative remains somewhat elliptical; as readers, we have the impression of piecing together the information our author gives us without being given the opportunity to grasp the entire clinical construction, or the clinical novelty unveiled by Freud. But another ingredient helps us consistent with what Freud presents to us: that the fantasy originates in early childhood before compulsory schooling. We later learn that the patient, deprived of examples encountered at school (i.e., the scenes of punishment), must nourish the material in another way to continue to sustain his fantasy. This will be the case with readings, which provide narratives from which the dreamer draws and updates his fantasy activity. Thus, on the one hand, the fantasy representation is very old, barely recoverable through speech, and on the other hand, it constantly needs to be updated, nourished by fresh news, almost ready-to-wear.

Freud states,

> The child began to compete with these works of fiction by producing his own phantasies and by constructing a wealth of situations and institutions, in which children were beaten, or were punished and disciplined in some other way, because of their naughtiness and bad behaviour.[3]

It is important not to lose track of what Freud is recounting: we are told that in the absence of real scenes, one must seek material in literature. But are we still talking about the same thing? Does the "patient" read *Uncle Tom's Cabin* in the hope of finding almost "pornographic material" to masturbate to, or is this now another activity, less eroticized, more nuanced, perhaps even more sublimated? Well, we learn from Freud that this is not the case and that the new material has changed in nature. But what exactly is it about? On occasion, the subject, confronted with real scenes that might involve moments of flogging, derives no satisfaction from them. He or she might even feel a certain repulsion or aversion or, in some cases, find these scenes unbearable. Freud even specifies, "Moreover, it was always a condition of the more sophisticated phantasies of later years that the punishment should do the children no serious injury." In other words, we are in the realm of pretense and pantomime.

According to Freud's reconstruction of the fantasy, a certain pantomime must be respected to such an extent that there might be an "inversely proportional" relationship between the invented fantasy and the real punishments experienced by the child. Even if this hypothesis cannot be corroborated, it says a lot about how Freud relates these two necessarily heterogeneous elements of fantasy: "the individuals from whom the data for these analyses were derived were very seldom beaten in their childhood, or were at all events not brought up by the help of the rod." We can see how the fantasy in question—from the moment of its origin—is indeed a fantasy in every sense of the word, as Freud considers it to be an invented artifact, a fiction.

Why on earth should there be a prehistory to the fantasy representation, to the point that Freud insists on its occurrence during preschool age? It is as if Freud recognized the somewhat headless aspect of the fantasy and, puzzled, he sought precision at all costs: "who was the beaten child? The author of the fantasy himself or another child? . . . Who was it that beat the child? An adult? But who exactly?" Freud adds, "nothing could be ascertained that threw any light upon all these questions—only the hesitant reply, 'I know nothing more about it: a child is being beaten.⁴'" The only enlightening response from the patient seemed to concern the gender of the beaten child: "always only boys."

But let us not lose sight of the subtitle of Freud's text, which indeed concerns the genesis of perversions. Again, nothing is decided, according to Freud, in the sense that the fantasy of being beaten—surprisingly frequent (sic)—does not necessarily produce sexual perversions. Freud explains, in a rather predictable way, that the infantile fantasy can have different fates, depending on whether it is subjected to repression or sublimation. Conversely, in people inclined to perverse practices— among them, according to Freud, inversion (homosexuality) or fetishism—one might assume that an anamnesis would reveal the existence of such a fantasy on which the pervert has been fixated since childhood. There is a cause-and-effect link between the fantasy of being beaten and deviant sexual behavior.

A Freudian Reconstruction of the Fantasy

As in the structural analysis of myths, one must consider the fantasy not as a fixed block but rather as the product of a series of changes that Freud does not hesitate to refer to as transformations (*Wandlungen*). To engage in such an analysis, Freud warns that he will limit himself to female cases (which happen to form the majority of his clinical sample). Freud is therefore about to reconstruct the fantasy— hypothetically present since early childhood (between ages 2 and 6)—by breaking it down into different phases. The first phase, as is well-known, is that which can be expressed with the phrase "a child is being beaten." To this are added two clarifications: first, the child is never the author of the fantasy (if one can even speak of an author), and second, the one who does the beating is always an adult. Freud indicates, "Later on this indeterminate grown-up person becomes recognizable clearly and unambiguously as the (girl's) *father*.⁵" Freud thus sums up the first phase with the proposition "*My father is beating the child*," but also adds that the child in question is "hated by me" ("My father is beating the child *whom I hate*.")

What should we make of this first phase and, more concretely, of this Freudian construction? As we have understood it, Freud permits himself to add two elements to the simple phrase "a child is being beaten": the father as the adult who performs the beating and the feeling of hatred toward the beaten child. This first phase only makes sense if it is related to a second phase, which Freud expresses as follows: "I am being beaten by the father" (*Ich werde vom Vater geschlagen*). This statement, however, is never made by the analysand; it is a "construction" of the analysis (*Sie ist eine Konstruktion der Analyse*) and, obviously, it never took place in real life (*sie habe niemals eine reale Existenz gehabt*) and yet remains nonetheless a necessity (*aber darum nicht minder eine Notwendigkeit*).

We know that Freud calls the type of interpretation that must be practiced in analysis a "construction"; even if the analysand has never uttered these statements as such, these constructions are no less a necessity of the analysis, elements without which it could not progress. However, one can rightly ask whether such or such a construction is relevant, or whether they are really appropriate, necessary, vital even, for the analysis. Another detail: how can Freud be so sure that the second phase, where it is the father who beats, *habe niemals eine reale Existenz gehabt* ("never had any real existence")? We must keep these elements in mind so that they may be taken up again later on in our commentary.

Regarding the potentially arbitrary nature of constructions in analysis (constructions that are generally communicated to the analysand), it is the third phase of the fantasy that will set us on the path to a perhaps questionable management of the cure—possibly the product of the analyst's prejudices or even of their counter-transference (in the sense Lacan gives to the term). Indeed, according to Freud, the third phase resembles the first in the sense that the statement becomes again what it originally was—namely, it remains indeterminate since "the person who beats is never the father" or is, at most, a "teacher (*Lehrer*)." Given that the fantasy returns to its original form—simply, "a child is being beaten"—and, considering that it is Freud who elaborates the rest of the constructions mentioned earlier, has never been anything else for the analysand, what ultimately happens is expressed by the latter in the following words (which might be the cherry on top): "*Auf eindringliches Befragen äußern die Patienten nur: Ich schaue wahrscheinlich zu.*" We can translate the phrase as, "In response to a persistent inquiry (sic) the patients merely say, "*Ich schaue wahrscheinlich zu*," meaning "I am probably looking on.⁶"

Of course, the phrase "I am probably looking on" highlights the subject's position—their being somewhere an enjoyer of this scene and thus inevitably involved in it (let us not forget that these are erotic scenes involving masturbation). Nevertheless, Freud's patient is cornered by the analyst's questioning, which does not let up. Fundamentally, the patient has nothing more to add concerning the fantasy she has brought up except that 1) a child is being beaten (in the third phase, importantly, it involves many children—*viele Kinder*—and always boys) and 2) the one who does the beating is not a child but an adult. I understand that this way of summarizing things might seem arbitrary, but let's temporarily assume that this is the essence of the fantasy that interests us, its minimal skeleton as it is presented by the analysand.

The Enigma of the Second Phase

It is clear that the second phase of the fantasy is never remembered by the patient and that it is a construction of the analyst. It is the repressed itself—the child is beaten by the father. Freud informs us, however, that in just one case, a male patient remembers this second phase in the course of the analysis and brings up a scene where it is the mother who beats the child and, subsequently, other women resembling the mother (such as the mothers of school friends).

But is this example relevant? Since it is the mother who does the beating (or the mother's substitutes), and since this is an erotic and onanistic fantasy, can it be considered a "repressed second phase" as Freud presents it in his text? This is uncertain. Concerning the second phase—the fruit of a construction in the analysis—we can assume it is invented by Freud and thus also constructed on the basis of his own prejudices. What prompts us to think this way? The fact that the fantasy is constructed based on the hypothesis of the Oedipus complex. Indeed, part III of "A Child is Being Beaten" ends with the observation that the reconstruction of the three phases of the fantasy "have so far remained quite unintelligible." To remedy this, Freud attempts to explain the aforementioned series of transformations, and yet we nevertheless end up with only one reconstructed, invented, and patched together stage: the second phase.

Both the first phase ("a child (whom I hate) is being beaten (by the father)") and the third, ("many children" are beaten "by adults") are more or less the patient's contribution. It is only the second phase that operates a transformation, since the subject does not occupy the same place—their subjective position changes. They are not the agent of the punishment, but rather its passive object. We can imagine that if Freud takes the male case as an example—whereas at the beginning of the text, he emphasizes the majority of women with the same fantasy—it is because he is quite alone with the fantasy of the female analysands. Could the male case have helped him understand the second phase in the female patients?

In his article, Freud reasons in the following way: "With boys the wish to beget a child from their mother is never absent, with girls the wish to have a child by their father is equally constant." It is clear that Freud analyzes the fantasy "a child is being beaten" through the prism of the Oedipus complex, with a natural distribution of sexual preferences (thus of object choice): as the thread is to the needle, the girl is to the boy. Thanks to Oedipal logic—because in the boy, unlike the girl, there would be a reversal—Freud can construct the famous second phase: the boy was active (desiring his own mother), and now he has become passive (being beaten by her). If the boy had remained "active"—becoming "sadistic" for example—there would have been no reversal, in which case it would not have helped Freud at all in his construction of the enigmatic second phase of the female cases: "I am beaten by the father." It is evident how much Freud struggles here with the theoretical construction of the fantasy.

"Anna and Her Sisters"

We might add a new case to Freud's clinical casuistry, that of "Anna." Indeed, Anna Freud, Freud's daughter, underwent two rounds of analysis with her father. This may seem strange today, but it was considerably less so at the beginning of the twentieth century. Not that such a practice didn't arouse curiosity at the time—far from it. The circumstances of this choice, by both Freud and Anna, are subject to several hypotheses, but the fact remains that this choice was made.

Why does this seem relevant when studying the notion of fantasy in psychoanalysis? Let me state this outright: I hypothesize that Freud's concept of fantasy, particularly in the established form that emerges from "A Child is Being Beaten," comes directly from Anna's analysis. Moreover, a well-known text by Anna Freud—the one that allowed her to become a member of the Vienna Psychoanalytic Society—serves as the necessary complement to the only valid understanding of "A Child is Being Beaten." I propose to demonstrate this necessary complementarity based on the following hypothesis: Anna Freud's text allows us to better grasp what is at stake in "A Child is Being Beaten" than her father's does. If this hypothesis is pertinent, I will need to elucidate the reasons why the daughter's text clarifies certain obscure areas of the text by the father of psychoanalysis.

Anna Freud, as mentioned, underwent two rounds of analysis with Freud, the first from the autumn of 1918 to May of 1920, and the second from 1922 to 1925. Little is known about what may have motivated this process, although the figure of Lou Andreas-Salomé, with whom Anna had strong ties, played an important role. What is known, however, is the framework of this analytical treatment: it involved five or six sessions per week, mostly in the evening, sometimes very late (around 9 or 10 pm).

Anna apparently exhibited some symptoms, including, it seems, questioning and hesitation in choosing a profession. But what interests us most is the step she took in 1922, when, on May 31st of that year, she presented a paper to become a member of the Vienna Psychoanalytic Society. Her presentation was published in the journal *Imago* in Vienna that same year under the title "Beating fantasies and Daydreams.[7]" One can immediately see from the title that the author relates two seemingly distinct elements: the fantasy described by Freud and the fantasy activity that Freud early on called "daydreaming." To avoid unnecessary suspense, I will say outright that it is very likely that the case presented by Anna Freud is her own.

If so, one must understand that this was still the heroic era of psychoanalysis when analysts often used themselves as examples of clinical cases. Moreover, Anna gave this presentation in order to become a member of a psychoanalytic society, so it could be seen as a sort of "entry pass" before the term existed.

Anna Freud's Text

Since this was an oral presentation, the text begins with a "Ladies and Gentlemen," except that, as Fernand Cambon[8] very pertinently notes, the phrase seems to have been reversed, as Anna Freud supposedly said *Meine Herren und Damen* (instead of the usual *Meine Damen und Herren*). One might wonder about the reasons for such a reversal, but one cannot but be surprised that she phrased it this way, especially since one of the key points of the fantasy studied by the future psychoanalyst involves a kind of inversion, even a masculine identification of the case presented.

Other details of the speech are curious, such as when at the beginning of her address, the young woman refers to the strict rules (*Ihre strengen Regeln*) of the psychoanalytic institution, only to later speak of the "institutions" fantasized about by the female case presented, where "rules and laws are established" (*stellt Regeln und Gesetze*) to punish children. There are still other significant details, such as when she explains that she is moving away from her position as an "idle spectator" to become more enterprising within the association—she declares that she knows the psychoanalytic institution does not approve of this idleness and that she obtained this information "from a reliable source," in clear allusion to her father.

Right from the start, Anna Freud informs her audience that this is a "small illustration" of "A Child is Being Beaten" and specifies that she owes much to Lou Andreas-Salomé, as the intervention she is about to read has been made possible by "a series of conversations" with her close friend. Indeed, Anna Freud quickly refers to her father's text on fantasy, but just as quickly she emphasizes the importance of daydreams for women presenting a masochistic fantasy of "being beaten," which often leads them to forsake sexual satisfaction by renouncing masturbation. This aspect is mentioned by Freud, even if it doesn't occupy as much space in his writing, as he seems to refer to two of the cases he dealt with:

> In two of my four female cases an elaborate superstructure [*Überbau*] of daydreams, which was of great significance for the life of the person concerned, had grown up over the masochistic beating phantasy. The function of this superstructure was to make possible a feeling of satisfied excitation, even though the masturbatory act was abstained from. In one of these cases the content—being beaten by the father—was allowed to venture again into consciousness, so long as the subject's own ego [*Ich*] was made unrecognizable by a thin disguise. The hero of these stories was invariably beaten (or later only punished, humiliated, etc.) by his father.[9]

This latter remark by Freud is doubly interesting, not only because it complements his text with a clinical example where, as he had already stated, the victim of a woman's fantasy is a man, but also because of two possibilities it opens up: either Freud and his daughter followed the same patient (the one reported by Anna), or Anna herself is the subject of the communication, as the case she presents resembles the example given by Freud.

The case reported by Anna is centered on the importance of daydreams and the transformations they undergo, and this is where her contribution's originality lies. Notably however, the key point concerns the correlation between this fantasy activity, these daydreams, and the fantasy of "being beaten" (we will see that Anna often uses the expression "being beaten" instead of the famous "a child is being beaten"). She begins, therefore, with a description of the case, a description that closely follows her father's guidelines: it is a girl who, at the age of five or six, in any case before school age, constructs a fantasy with very "monotonous" content (a term used by Freud in his text)—"any boy is beaten by any adult." To this, Anna adds, "A little later, it transforms into: 'Many boys are beaten by many adults.'"

What I am interested in pointing out is not only how her remarks align with Freud's (let us remember: *viele Kinder*, many children, constitute the third phase described by Freud), but also how, the way Anna describes it, one moves directly from the first to the last phase of the fantasy construction. It is important to note this, in the sense that there are no well-distinguished "stages" in the real case, since these stages are invented or reconstructed by Freud. Furthermore, Anna subscribes to the incomprehensible aspect of these stories, as her father describes them ("they are only reported in sparse terms and without the slightest clarity"). And Anna concludes, "Each one of the scenes she fantasied, frequently only very briefly, was accompanied by strong sexual excitement and terminated in a masturbatory act.[10]"

That said, it would be worthwhile to dwell a bit more on a very significant point explained by Anna Freud, which is the fact that both the formula "a child is being beaten" and its pluralization into "many children" are characterized by anonymity: we do not know who these children or these adults are. Though not stated in these exact terms, it is almost as if the faces of the people in question were blurred. This is symptomatic, as if they were wearing masks. From this we can conclude, along with Freud and his daughter, that this is material to be interpreted; the face of the beaten child is that of the subject, and the face of the adult who is doing the beating is that of the father. And here we simply have the famous "second phase" as it is recreated by Freud, but we see that it is not about phases and scansions but is rather an interpretation. For Freud, in order for an interpretation to truly be an interpretation, it must involve Oedipus: not only does the father do the beating (since here we're talking about a majority of female cases), but these blows are merely translating the father's love, as dictated by Oedipus.

As I proposed, the originality of Anna Freud's presentation also lies in the emphasis on daydreams—that is, a kind of fantasy devoid of its sexual component, in which this erotic aspect is not absent at all—far from it—but is rather attenuated.

Thus, in the case presented by Freud's daughter, there is a shift from the fantasy of being beaten to daydreams, moving toward a "sublimated" form, as Anna specifies. Before this, other "transformations" take place (the word transformation is often used in the presentation), such as the invention of institutions with "strict rules," where decisions are made on how to punish children. But the essential point lies in the transformation of the narrative, which shifts toward a plurality of stories drawn from literature or inspired by it and containing a multiplicity of scenarios that, Anna says, "offer the same structure." But how did we get here?

Fantasy and the Ego

Let's go back for a moment. On the one hand, we have the fantasy of being beaten with its internal variations, so to speak, starting with the singular and ending with the plural. On the other hand, Oedipus or not, the important aspect in Freud's interpretation lies in the permutation of the fantasy agent, moving from being a mere spectator to becoming the object of punishment. The shift from the position of observing pleasure-seeker to object of torment is a condition for the transition from singular to plural, from one to many.

Anna says that the fantasy of "being beaten" becomes less frequent over time and that the source of pleasure it grants the fantasizer becomes increasingly imperfect because it is too mixed with shame and guilt. And so, "at the same time" (when the fantasy of being beaten becomes rare)—"this could have occurred between the eighth and tenth years"—the child begins a new type of fantasy activity, an activity that "she herself called 'nice stories' in contrast to the ugly beating fantasy.[11]" This pair of opposites—beautiful/not beautiful—is important because it inaugurates a whole series of oppositions that nourish daydreams, as we will see. What makes up these nice stories? They involve a multitude of invented stories based on the dreamer's current reality, in which she has an "altruistic, kind, and benevolent" attitude,—another opposition to the position of being a complicit observer (already complicit by way of the masturbation that accompanied the imagined scene) of the fantasy of being beaten, always applied to other children and never to herself. She draws her material from stories she reads but also, undoubtedly, from things she experiences in reality because, as Anna Freud points out, these nice stories do not conflict with reality; we can even assume that they are part of it:

> All the figures in these nice stories had names, individual faces, external appearances that were detailed with great exactness, and personal histories which frequently reached far back into their fantasied past. The family circumstances of these figures, their friendships and acquaintances, and their relationship to each other were precisely specified and al incidents in their daily life were fashioned as true to reality as possible. The setting of the story readily changed with every change in the life of the daydreamer, just as she frequently incorporated bits and pieces of events she had read about.[12]

Thus, this fantasy activity involves multiple parallel, "continued stories" that are unrelated to each other. What does this kind of direct connection between imagined beautiful stories and reality inspire in us? What can we say about this relationship between fantasy and reality with (almost) no discontinuity? The answer seems simple: we can note that the fantasy (daydream) corresponds perfectly with the self, and in the same way, we can put the specular self (which Lacan writes as i(a)), the ideal self, and the fantasy—the $ \$ <> a $ which the psychoanalyst places on the same right side in his famous "graph of desire"—in an equivalent relationship. This ideal image of the self (let's recall: altruism, kindness, benevolence) is more ideal the more it is devoid of sexual activity (onanism) that generates shame and guilt.

Transformations

The question to resolve now is, "To what extent are we authorized to see this—these daydreams—as a construction based on the masochistic fantasy of 'being beaten'?" A key additional point in understanding the daydreams is that the dreamer "experienced a pleasure identical or even superior to that of the fantasy itself." This is a good definition of the Lacanian notion of *plus-de-jouir* ("surplus enjoyment"), this excess or "bonus" of pleasure provoked by daydreams.

Here, then, is the kernel of the nice stories our dreamer imagined: she is 14 or 15 years old, reading "a boy's book in the style of *Guten Kameraden*." From this literary material "for boys," she invents stories where, essentially, the scenario is as follows: a young nobleman "aged 15, a boy who is therefore the same age as the dreamer" is imprisoned in a castle where he endures confinement. This, says Anna Freud, constitutes "the external framework," and within this framework, numerous small stories unfold, independent of one another, with variations, up until the moment of "climax." The daydreams are often limited to two main actors: a wicked, dark, and violent adult who can be sometimes harsh, sometimes benevolent, granting favors to the second character—namely, the 15-year-old boy, who by definition is good, faithful, etc. The adult (a burgrave) sometimes "almost tortures" the boy but ultimately lets him escape. Sometimes the boy commits a transgression and the adult catches him but forgives the public humiliation that would have ensued. Anna clarifies, "In each of these, it is in a state of full excitement that the dreamer experiences the anxiety and endurance of the threatened boy. At the moment when the anger and rage of the tormentor turn into pity and kindness, that is, at the climax of each scene, this excitement resolves into a pure feeling of pleasure." One might even say that sometimes the tormentor and the victim are one and the same person, a striking aspect that undoubtedly helped Anna Freud conceive of a defense mechanism: identification with the aggressor—understood in her case to be a man.

Anna Freud, the Structuralist

It is surprising to perceive something very close to structuralism in Anna Freud's writing process and even in her vocabulary. The very fact of bringing together manifestly different stories (daydreams) under the same framework speaks volumes about how she perceived her studied object. Additionally, Anna Freud considers that all these stories have "the same structure" (*nämliche Gerüst*). She insists, "Every one of the individual scenes of the other so-called 'nice stories' had, with only a few variations, the same structure.[13]" (*Das ist übrigens mit geringen Variationen auch die Struktur*) to which all the "nice stories" are reduced. To conclude, she writes, "It is in this structure (*In dieser Struktur*) that the unexpected analogy of the nice stories with the fantasy of 'being beaten' lies." Freud's daughter speculates that the fantasy, in its formal structure, also involves an opposition between adults and children or between the strong and the weak; it is in this that there is an equivalence between the nice stories and the fantasy of being beaten. The only difference, she thinks, lies in their respective resolutions: in the fantasy there is punishment, whereas in the daydreams there is "forgiveness and reconciliation." This structural identity was finally revealed in the analysis by the fact that the fantasy of "being beaten" interrupts the daydream, the nice story.

The following comment made by the young Anna Freud is worth quoting here, striking in its precision and intelligence:

> The examination of the interdependence between the fantasy of 'being beaten' and the nice stories already gives us three important relations between them: first, a striking analogy in structure (*Analogie in der Struktur*) of each isolated fragment; secondly, a series of internal overdeterminations; thirdly, the possibility of a direct passage from one to the other.

This last point is crucial because not only does it imply the aforementioned irruption of the fantasy of being beaten in the middle of a nice story, but it also provides the key to the movements of progression and regression between the fantasy and the nice stories. Again I'll quote Anna Freud, who at this point in her presentation refers back to her father's text:

> As already mentioned, Freud says that the form ni which we know the beating fantasy is not the original one, but si a substitute for an incestuous love scene that distorted by repression and regression to the anal-sadistic phase finds expression as a beating scene. This point of view suggests an explanation of the difference between beating fantasy and daydream: what appears to be an advance from beating fantasy to nice story si nothing but a return to an earlier phase.[14]

In other words, the "apparent progress" is a regression. This last comment is all the more interesting since as the reader probably knows, the notions of progression and regression, particularly in a topological context, are also very present in Lacan. Let us recall the following remark by Lacan on the Dora case: "That it is true, as Freud thinks, that the return to a passionate complaint about the father represents a regression when compared with the relations that had begun to develop with Herr K.[15]"

In other words, Anna Freud sees that these nice stories, which she considers a form of "sublimation," actually constitute at the same time a regression—both in terms of their Oedipal tone and a narcissistic regression to the specular register, the same one that makes the dreamer amiable, altruistic, etc. Nevertheless, the essential trait to highlight is that the dreamer "dreams herself up" as a boy, as even a superficial reading of the clinical case shows. I do not completely reject the hypothesis of sublimation because if by any chance the clinical case presented by Anna was indeed a testimony of her analysis, one perceives that virile identification is for her a form of sublimation. The hypothesis is even further validated if the Freudian concept of sublimation is illuminated by the notion of the *sinthome*, a concept advocated by Lacan in the 1970s that was to be related to character, what for Freud translates the unanalyzable by definition. Thus, sublimation would have occurred in the dreamer, probably when she realized something about her own castration, around "14 or 15 years old," as does the "young homosexual woman" studied by Freud in a text published in 1921, during the time he was analyzing Anna.

The Anna Case Is Also the Freud Case

If the case of Dora was, according to Serge Cottet, somehow the "case of Freud[16]" what can be said about the case of Anna, analyzed by her own father? One of the cases reported in the text written by Freud two months after Anna's presentation, "Remarks on Dream Interpretation," raises our suspicion. In the text, the expression "continued story" is used—the same expression employed by Anna in her presentation before the Vienna Psychoanalytic Society:

> In some analyses, or in some periods of an analysis, a divorce may become apparent between dream life and waking life, like the divorce between the activity of phantasy [*Phantasietätigkeit*] and waking life which is found in the 'continued story'2 (a novel in daydreams). In that case one dream leads off from another, taking as its central point some element which was lightly touched upon in its predecessor, and so on. But we find far more frequently that dreams are not attached to one another but are interpolated into a successive series of portions of waking thought.[17]

The question Freud addresses is dream interpretation, which had already been the subject of other texts and lectures. The text, written in July, takes as its pretext a new edition of *The Interpretation of Dreams*, which is why Freud focuses on examples of dreams that either should not be interpreted or that the analysand should be left to interpret themselves. Here is how Freud begins part IX of this new text on dreams; the example he gives cannot but intrigue us:

> Here is an extract from the dream of a girl with a strong fixation to her father, who had difficulty in talking during the analysis. She was sitting in a room with a girl friend, and dressed only in a kimono. A gentleman came in and she felt

embarrassed. But the gentleman said: 'Why, this is the girl we saw once before dressed so nicely!'—The gentleman stood for me, and, further back, for her father. But we can make nothing of the dream unless we make up our mind to replace the most important element in the gentleman's speech with its contrary: 'This is the girl I saw once before *undressed* and who looked so nice then!' When she was a child of three or four she had for some time slept in the same room as her father and everything goes to suggest that she used then to throw back her clothes in her sleep to please her father. The subsequent repression of her pleasure in exhibiting herself was the motive for her secretiveness in the treatment, her dislike of showing herself openly.[18]

The case summoned by Freud needs no further comment. I can only make note of the following details: the presence of the English expression ("continued story") used by Anna in her presentation, the case of a young girl in love with her father who would have read the *History of an Infantile Neurosis* and who reads "her own case, printed" in the dream (the text for the *Imago* journal?), and, finally, the misalliance with the male gender, not to mention the presence of a friend (dis)robed in a kimono. . . . Anna Freud's text ends with these words that, referring to the patient whose case is presented, make note of the intertwining of statement and enunciation:

> The written story treats al parts of the content of the daydream as equally objective material, the selection being guided solely by regard for their suitability for representation. For the better she succeeds in the presentation of her material, the greater will be the effect on others and therefore also her own indirect pleasure gain. By renouncing her private pleasure in favor of making an impression on others, the author has accomplished an important developmental step: the transformation of an autistic into a social activity. We could say: she has found the road that leads from her fantasy life back to reality.[19]

The case of Anna is undoubtedly also the case of Freud in that it includes what was un-analyzed in him, such as his prejudices, his countertransference, and his attachment to Oedipus (understood as sexual normativity). Dora, the young homosexual, and Anna: in all three cases, an obstacle remains like an insurmountable rock, likely a correlate of the common prejudice that in humans there is a "sexual relationship." It can certainly be argued that Anna Freud fostered multiple encounters with women throughout her life; with these sisters, or soul sisters, she shared in an intimate understanding, continuing the daydreams of her adolescence.

Dialectic Identified by Anna Freud, between Fantasy and Daydream

Figure 4.1, which I already used in Chapter 2, is to the fantasy of "being beaten" (libidinal reserve) what 2 is to the "beautiful stories" (daydreams). One can see in

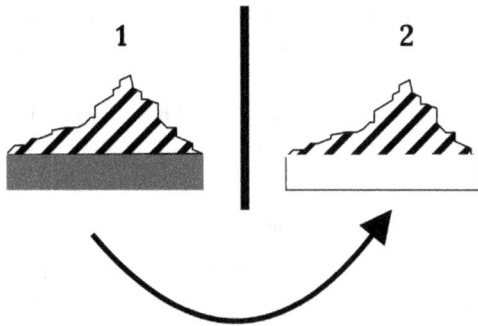

Figure 4.1 The libidinal reserve.

this simplified version of Lacan's optical diagram—which I use here to enrich my reading of Anna Freud's text—that the image in the mirror (hence the daydream) in 2 conceals the libidinal reserve deployed by the fantasy of "being beaten" in 1.

The Fantasy and the Object a

After this parenthesis on "A Child is Being Beaten" and Anna Freud's wonderful commentary, I now attempt to return to our discussion of the object a. What is the relationship between fantasy, daydreaming, and what Lacan calls the "object of objects"—the main subject of this book? First, we must situate (-φ), or symbolic castration—a function that must remain hidden as such. This (-φ)—what allows Anna's patient to fantasize, "dream," or engage in daydreams—is related to Lacan's libidinal reserve, and if I have repeatedly emphasized this concept, it is because (-φ) renders evident a certain correspondence with castration in the imaginary sense. This is why Lacan, after dealing with the radicality of this (-φ) in his seminar on anxiety, seemingly retraces his steps and speaks of "the form of castration" as if he were speaking of the "commodity form"—that is, "castration in its imaginary structure." In an attempt to articulate in clear terms the importance of the "traumatic scene," or the relation to the sexual, Lacan goes on to claim that this (-φ) exists "at the level of the break that occurs in the approach to the libidinal image of the similar." If he can assert that there is no relation to the other sex, it is above all because there inevitably must be another sex, for example in the form of the traumatic scene.

Thus, in the face of this imaginary instance of castration, Lacan proposes the existence of a kind of pseudo-reflexivity that he calls fantasy. To be clear, this movement—this distancing, pseudo-reflexive instance—is not due to the very form of castration (imaginary) but is rather caused by (-φ), by the *Spaltung* introduced by the symbolic. Since the other contains within it this fundamental dissatisfaction linked to the drive that we have discussed in previous chapters, then (-φ) is already in the other (let us recall the (-φ) drawn by Lacan in place of the other, in his simplified schema of the inverted bouquet). In other words, the other is assimilated to desire, except that desire itself disassimilates this other, rendering it insufficient: (-φ.) This is where the other comes to show traces of the uncanny, of anxiety, or of a non-assimilation proper to desire. But what happens through fantasy? In what way is it a response to (-φ)? And if it is, what kind of response is it?

From Anxiety to Love and Back

Anxiety and love seem to be two sides of the same coin. They are two modalities that relate to the object a. As I have mentioned, according to Lacan, anxiety is an example of a manifestation of the object a. This object is not an object but rather a function that translates desire in the being subjected to structure; this desire, insofar as it is necessarily a ternary mediation with the world (of signifiers that represent), is what produces an indirect relationship to the objects of the world. While we might imagine the subject as a being in relation to other subjects and objects (after all, why not conceive of it this way, in a subject–object relationship?), something (a "signal," Lacan would say, following Freud) comes to indicate that this relationship is not quite right, that something complicates a mechanism that one previously imagined to be well-oiled and self-evident (subject-object relationship). Some little snag comes to trouble the one who thought they were autonomous. Truth be told, I could summarize this very book with the following formula: the living being is not autonomous and is even, and especially, an "object" (this would also help us to not compulsively use the word "subject" in place of "person," "child," "analysand," "patient," etc.).

With regard to anxiety, the terms signal and affect have undoubtedly been well chosen in the sense that they indicate that it is not linked to the signifier and precisely escapes the signifier that is supposed to represent the living being. For if, on the one hand, the living being is shielded from excess (why not say affective?) or loss of control by symbolic castration—by the incidence of the symbolic (-φ)—on the other hand, the signifier can never completely reduce jouissance to the erogenous rim (jouissance in the sense of a kind of disturbance), if only because of the very structure of the signifier, its being "ternary" rather than univocal (which might make us believe that each thing would have a corresponding signifier).

If the symbolic ensured this kind of univocality, psychoanalysis wouldn't need to exist—it would not be necessary. For us, the unconscious is essentially the fact of the structure called symbolic: it is equivocal and produces an annihilation of the referent (real, material) as such. Let us think for a moment about what happens in autism, where the word is not at all the murder of the thing but, on the contrary, the thing (or even things) that produces words that allow the autistic person to speak. But can these words represent them? If there is anxiety in autism, it is often linked to the word itself, which functions as a thing that triggers all sorts of phenomena, including physical ones. For the subject to be represented by the signifier, they must be anticipated by this signifier; for example, they must speak before even knowing what they are saying; this is the very structure of speech in the speaking being.

In his seminar on anxiety, Lacan speaks about love in order to explain that there is a close relationship between the two. I analyze this issue by studying the notion of "passage to the act." In the passage to the act, as defined by Lacan, there is a sort of flattening of the signifying dialectic, or the signifying trajectory as such, through which the subject manages to represent themselves, albeit imperfectly. The close relationship between passage to the act, love, and object a allows Lacan to explore the notions of love and identification. To follow him here, we must begin with a question very dear to Lacan—namely, "the relationship of being to having."

This relation is clarified when Lacan revisits topics addressed in his seminar on transference but also questions raised during the seminars on the object relation and the formations of the unconscious. In this latter seminar, Lacan explores the notion of identification and its relationship with mourning, revisiting Freud when he stipulates that during the mourning process, the love object becomes an object of identification; in *Group Psychology and the Analysis of the Ego*, Freud further suggests that a love object can become an object of identification. He takes the case of Dora as an example, where, according to him, the young patient identifies with her father through the symptom of coughing: "for instance, Dora imitated her father's cough.[20])" These possible subjective changes allow Lacan to organize the Freudian jungle and to conceptualize these subjective modifications in terms of permutation, of changes in the position of the living being in relation to its narcissistic objects.

Regarding the subjective changes I have just referred to, it is also important to consider Lacan's reading of Plato's *Symposium* and his conception of transference: what interests Lacan is understanding how one becomes desirous where one was once desired or loved. He thus relies on the Freudian equation in *Group Psychology and the Analysis of the Ego* (to clarify, Dora, through a kind of regression, goes from loving her father to identifying with him) to formulate the question as follows: "how is it that a, the object of identification, also a, the object of love?[21]" As we can see, the question is posed in reverse, but this does not change Lacan's point of view.

Let us pause for a moment to focus on the preceding statements. The process highlighted by Lacan—where one goes from having to being and vice versa—is used to understand the subjective changes that lead to complete symbolization and the formation of a personality (although the word personality is debatable: Wallon assumes it to be constituted by the age of three, while Lacan considers that one does not have a complete personality before the age of twenty-five). The small child is everything that the other lacks (as long as the other loves them), but we know that they cannot remain indefinitely in this position of being loved for what they are; they must attempt to become what they are not (as long as they love). Except that, due to the mysteries of language and the symbolic, one can only be what one is not through having. The ego ideal, as conceived by Lacan and derived from Freudian formulations, is expressed in the transition from being to having:

from being to "lack of being." Or again, it is expressed in terms of being what one is not. The only remedy that being finds for being what it is not is having: Freud calls this neurosis.

If in love one passes from the *erômenos* to the *erastès*—from the beloved to the lover—it is because the *erastès* finds in the beloved something that could fulfill them: this is indeed the agalma of the other, of the beloved. This is particularly interesting when seen in the light of the diagrams proposed by Lacan and studied in the previous chapter. Our dear Dr. Lacan believes that there is a function of dreams in psychoanalysis that is related to awakening, insofar as the dream touches upon the real:

> The nucleus must be designated as belonging to the real—the real in so far as the identity of perception is its rule. . . . What does that mean, if not that as far as the subject is concerned, this is called awakening.[22]

This means that what we have studied regarding the body of the other as containing -ϕ—the fact that in the mirror image, we see nothing of this other—also, and perhaps especially, applies "to the waking state." Lacan writes,

> The world is all-seeing, but it is not exhibitionistic—it does not provoke our gaze. When it begins to provoke it, the feeling of strangeness begins too. What does that mean, if it not that, in the so-called waking state, there is an elision of the gaze, and an elision of the fact that not only does it look, it also shows. In the field of dreams, on the other hand, contrary, what characterizes the images is that *it shows*.[23]

Interestingly, in these remarks made in the commentary on a very well-known dream reported by Freud ("Father, don't you see, I'm burning?"), Lacan seeks to account for what happens not in the dream itself or in the state of wakefulness after the dream, but rather in what can happen between the two. This in-between state corresponds more or less to what we experience every morning when we wake up, except that not all of our wakings necessarily result in "awakening." What is awakening? It is something that changes the very nature of the one who dreams; they become the object, or the effect of the dream.

In the waking state, we do not see -ϕ in the sense that if one is not too disturbed, this -ϕ behaves as if the (a) it conceals does not exist. Rather, we have something like awakening, which precisely opposes the waking state: it is no longer the same state of affairs; we wake up just at the moment when it shows itself, or when we are no longer just a "voyeur" (the question is extensively discussed by Lacan in the seminar in question, which could be entirely summarized with the words "The triumph of the gaze over the eye").[24]

This pathway allows us to return to our couple of the lover and the beloved, for the beloved awakens to something. Moreover, they are too awakened, to the point of lacking sleep In the proper sense. If we take into account the phenomenon of jealousy—of which Marcel Proust was a kind of expert—and if we consider that it is one of the symptoms of the state of being in love, then we can perfectly understand that -φ gives way to a. This a is what cannot be seen according to the diagram of the inverted bouquet, but it begins to be seen both in the phenomenon of depersonalization (or other similar phenomena) and in the state of being in love ("where was she yesterday afternoon?", "why is he not on time for our rendezvous?", etc.). These states, which verge on a kind of madness without being psychoses, clearly indicate that a can start to be seen and felt to an unreasonable degree. In the phenomenology of jealousy, we see the notions of time and space being suspended, and this is how Kant's transcendental aesthetics cannot easily account for phenomena that do not obey its laws. In other words, it is in subjective states like that of being in love, "falling in love," and the inherent jealousy that ensues, that we observe moments either of awakening or of strangeness. These are states where one steps out of the typical familiarity of the waking state. Even if strangeness leads us back to what is familiar, it is with the understanding that the family contains within it what is "unsettling" (take, for example, the horror of incest). The unsettling is the cause of what is familiar and vice versa. We therefore see that psychoanalytic formulations are not just abstract and that we are dealing here with the concrete realities of lives as they are lived.

Change of Discourse

Love and anxiety are thus two terms linked to the function of object a. Here we will continue to explore the notion of love in its most radical form. In the 1970s, Lacan suggested that during each change of discourse, or each major subjective change, we are dealing with love. The formula is well-known to readers of the psychoanalyst: "there is some emergence of analytic discourse with each shift from one discourse to another. I am not saying anything else when I say that love is the sign that one is changing discourses.[25]"

We can therefore deduce that love is a "sign"—and anxiety a signal—of the change from one subjective regime or one discourse to another, and this may also happen during a cure. Why love? Because, contrary to what Freud imagines, it is not familiar, and it is not merely repetition (think of his view of the Oedipus complex as a repetition or even love as a repetition of a childhood love: the proof lies in his text on Jensen's *Gradiva*). It is, on the contrary, the sign that one is leaving the familiar territory (that is, the waking state or even the i(a)) to which we are all too accustomed, including in the symptom. Lacan thus emphasizes both the fact that "it shows" (*ça montre*) and the state of awakening to account for a possible change, for something that allows the being to become something other than what it is. This same logic applies to the process of the analytic cure, where there are also moments of awakening. One gives a sort of testimony of these moments of awakening in "the pass," another of Lacan's concepts.

Lacan introduces a possible shift, a passage, or a change of position in the neurotic in the sense of what can make neurotics anxious is that the world is not what they believe it to be—that is, the usual familiar world. Thus, they do not like love, or falling in love, which pulls them out of their daily life and into the circle of this lack, this little insignificant detail that is love—this "nothing much."

And what is lacking in the Other? It is (a), or what -φ is supposed to veil. As long as the -φ inherent in the other does not concern the libidinal reserve, everything is fine (or everything is bad, which amounts to the same thing); as long as -φ does not let a appear—a moment of strangeness insofar as it can modify one's subjective position—the subject does not really risk anything because they believe they "have it" (hence Lacan's idea of "making their castration what is lacking in the Other"). They are deprived neither in terms of the image they want to reflect to the other nor in their certainty of being able to become what they are not, which is one of the modalities of being that I indicated above. Lacan thus asks, "How a, object of identification, is also **a**, object of love?" but, in this regression, a remains what it is, an instrument. It is with what one is that one can have or not have, if I may say so."

These last words refer to the Lacanian vocabulary found in "Kant avec Sade," written precisely at the same time as the seminar on anxiety, where the importance of the notion of permutation is highlighted. But what should we understand from Lacan's declaration that I have just cited? He explains two movements (and it is not for nothing that I allow myself to refer my readers to the "Kant avec Sade" essay) that are inherent in every subjective change—namely, the movements of progression and regression to which I have already referred. He had already made particular use of these terms in the seminar *The Object Relation* in order to understand what happens both with the Dora case and with that of "the young homosexual," and he revisits these mechanisms again in the seminar on anxiety and in "Kant avec Sade." These advances form the basis of his proposal in 1969 concerning his theory of the "four discourses," where the change from one discourse to another occurs either by progression or by regression.

We have seen that the passage from love to identification is made, in Dora's case, by way of a regression. But this does not hide from us the opposite path, that of love, where one goes from being lovable to being a lover by way of a progression. In other words, if the passage from love to identification (from being to having) is made by regression, the passage from identification to love (from having to being) is made by progression. And if Dora's movement is made by regression, that of "the young homosexual" is made by progression, for the latter falls madly in love with a lady (a situation in which we can suppose that states like jealousy predominate). Finally, the other well-known progressive movement, where one manifestly goes from the state of being loved to that of the lover, is the example of Alcibiades, as discovered by Plato and Lacan. To put things succinctly, in love, the path goes from Dora to Alcibiades, or from regression to progression. Psychoanalysis, as Lacan conceives it, is well-positioned in our culture to teach us something about this path.

"Passage à l'acte"

In his seminar on anxiety, Lacan dwells on the imaginary register in order to introduce the object. And yet he returns to it, as I have explained in previous chapters, to grasp something of what he calls the real, which can be defined as what resists symbolization, or what does not fit into signifiers. And it is indeed through the notion of "passage à l'acte" that Lacan can grasp a clinical instrument that allows for understanding the different nature of the object a and its relationship to the real.

But this passage à l'acte, like the notion of acting-out that Lacan explores in the same seminar, cannot be established without a reference to the subjective changes I have just discussed, both those that occur in the realm of love or during a cure and those that occur in the process of identification, in terms of progression and regression. I say that there is a relationship between passage à l'acte and the afore-mentioned permutations but that they are not the same phenomenon. Permutation thus remains closely linked to the notions of passage à l'acte and acting-out insofar as they are both related to anxiety.

How can one not see that passage à l'acte shows an excess that is different from the symbolic register? Why else would Lacan have introduced, very early on, the notion of the real as what (always) returns to the same place? It goes without saying that one could always attempt to interpret an act—the problem is not there. What differentiates an act from the symptom (which always contains an uninterpretable core, not subject to the effects of a psychoanalytic interpretation) is that something in it separates from the symbolic chain against which it emerges.

Let's take the case studied by Freud, which Lacan refers to as the case of the young homosexual. The case is too well-known to recall its content, so I will limit myself to mentioning that the young girl is 18 years old and is brought in by her father to consult Freud after a sort of suicide attempt (she jumped off a bridge onto a railway track that was said to be disused). According to the usual interpretation, the young girl's action is the result of the furious look her father gave her upon seeing her with her beloved; in fact, what motivated her action was that the "lady" she was courting had told her that their meetings and exchanges would come to an end (precisely because of the father's disapproval). We know that Freud interprets the suicidal "letting oneself fall" (*niederkommen*) as a repressed desire to "get pregnant," for it is hardly necessary to recall that everything had changed for the young adolescent from the moment her own mother had had a child.

It is, however, essential to recall Lacan's analysis of the case. He had already dealt with Freud's case in his seminar *The Object Relation* to demonstrate how the symbolic and imaginary axes should not be confused: on one hand, there is the symbolic axis through which the girl was expecting a child from her father (which would be the normalizing, Oedipal situation, so to speak), and on the other hand, we have the imaginary axis, which translates into the father's function as reduced to the imaginary: not the function of someone who could "give one a child," for example, but rather an imaginary rival that the girl confronts and defies. Although Lacan does not return to this distinction in the seminar on anxiety, it is fundamen-tal, for it allows us to precisely understand two different subjective positions that map on to the two movements discussed earlier (progression and regression—to be brief, the former for the "Oedipal" situation, the latter for the aggressive relation-ship with the father).

However, it should be noted that in his review of the case, Lacan does not place any importance on the "*niederkommen*/letting fall" interpretation but instead critiques it. We were accustomed to the critique of the handling of transference in the case (*The Object Relation*, for example), but in the seminar on anxiety, our author goes to the very heart of this major (symbolic) interpretation of the word *niederkommen*, affirming that the word alone cannot suffice to understand the passage to the act. Lacan, pointing out that the passage to the act is the root, so to speak, of the relationship to speech and the symbolic. This fundamental idea brings us back—if my reader will allow it—to the window or square of our cognitive friend Baron-Cohen (he calls it a square whereas I perceive a window). It is the very frame that moves from desire—understood as the desire of the other, the place where things begin to make sense—to the conjunction with what can be signified and thus signified before the law. This is the relationship that Lacan questions with the *mise en abîme*, so to speak, of the passage à l'acte, where the subject itself can be reduced to a—that is, that thing he hangs from in the gaze of the other as the place where desire clings to the law, or to the possibility of life symbolized as such.

And Acting Out?

I will limit myself here to recalling the distinction made by Lacan between "passage à l'acte" and "acting out." Why is this distinction important? Apart from the technical consequences, it seems to me that this distinction is crucial if we want to grasp what is at stake in inversion and permutation.

Lacan defines acting out as the moment when the subject identifies with a. In other words, in those moments of suspension related to something enigmatic in the desire of the Other, it is as if we are seeking meanings "from the gaze of the Other." It is enough to think of the child turning around to seek the assent of the Other— assent that as everyone knows, does not mean consent. Assent here would signify "the place of the witness" to what is happening, which is why Lacan believes that the entire first part of the story, where the young homosexual courts the Lady under the gaze of the Father (whether this gaze of the Father is embodied by the Father or not is not the issue), corresponds precisely to "acting out."

Let's consider this but without forgetting the inversion that I have already highlighted. The passage à l'acte, on the other hand, is of a completely different nature: "it is the confrontation of desire and law." Because it seems crucial to me, I'll clarify this point with Lacan's statement on acting out: "the gaze of the Father. It is through this that she feels definitively identified with 'a.'" In its total dependence on the ego ideal, the subject "made (a)," so to speak, is embodied here by the gaze. But "at the same time, rejected, ejected, off the stage. And this, only letting go, letting oneself fall, can achieve." Interestingly, in the first instance we have the almost imaginary strategy of the subject reducing itself to a, while the second instance— the passage à l'acte—is of a completely different nature, as there are no longer any strategies to deploy (no more inversions) and it has, so to speak, no more credit.

In the passage à l'acte, desire and law are no longer the same thing, and this is why one must change the framework, or modify one's repertoire.

We will need to make a necessary detour to understand the object a, and this detour is made through the concept of fantasy in its three aspects (symbolic, real, and imaginary) as it is elaborated by Jacques-Alain Miller in an unpublished course. In a certain way, fantasy must be thought of through the mechanisms of progression and regression that I have discussed in a non-exhaustive but I hope precise manner. One only has to reflect on the moments of progression and regression of Anna in her fantasy. Fantasy is what allows one to be subjected to a signifying framework and at the same time distance oneself from it by relying on what, by structure, is not signifying—namely the object a and what connects it to the real understood as non-symbolizable and for which "identity of perception is its rule."

In some respects, the structure (and therefore the unconscious) is a salutary creation, as it allows for the existence of a certain rigid framework—the fantasy. Indeed, if we take the example of Anna Freud's "beautiful stories" in which she represents herself as a boy, we see a whole series of significant oppositions unfold (old/young; strong/weak; good/evil, etc.). Yet this structure is also not complete without a relation to what seems to escape the signifier; something is missing from the structure. To put it differently, life inhabits the structure and thus shapes it through libido. The element that should interest us most, however, is highlighted by Lacan when he stipulates that,

> the neurotic recoils from making his castration something positive, namely the guarantee of the function of the Other, this Other who slips away in the indefinite deferral of meanings, this Other where the subject no longer sees itself as destiny, but destiny that has no end.

This is precisely where the young homosexual did not recoil. Concerning the neurotic (let's admit that our young homosexual is not a prime example of neurosis), it is worth highlighting both the paradox and the reversal at stake in Lacan's statement about the word "destiny": a destiny that has no end is not a destiny. In Greek mythology, destiny has an end that is known in advance except that it escapes the will of its hero—it is decided by others. The modern neurotic, who is anything but Greek, must invent a destiny for himself, must even choose a destiny, except that again, a destiny that one chooses is not a destiny. This means that 1) the neurotic does not decide his destiny, and 2) because his destiny has no end, he must invent it for himself. In short, Hamlet is not Oedipus. Or, to put it another way, the neurotic is divided, but he is also responsible for his own division, without which analysis would not be necessary.

Let's take another example of what psychoanalysis might call the fantasy: the woman (let's continue defaming her) as the emblem and privileged representation of the libidinal reserve, a reserve that draws on the object of desire and is marked by the $(-\varphi)$. Let's assume that our obsessive neurotic is in love with a woman and is magnetized by the following fantasy, which could be (and should be) reduced to the phrase "one fucks a woman."

This would be a funnier version of the fantasy "a child is being beaten," except that J.-A. Miller already deduced it from the case of President Schreber. The woman in question indeed embodies the enjoyment that the male neurotic can only suppose. But a problem arises: since she embodies the fucked, joyous woman, she escapes him as such because she could be fucked by other men (and it is this possibility that this indeed nourishes the fantasy). We can recognize here how the symptom of jealousy is directly linked to the fantasized statement "one fucks a woman" (as with Freud, the symptom is always linked to the fantasy). The "one fucks a woman" could never imply only the neurotic himself; the "one" is instead there to show the imaginary multiplication in which he sees himself through various rivals. In this regard, it is worth mentioning the case of a young man with a fantasy of this order who pretends that his girlfriend is responsible for the fantasy. Two sessions after having stated the fantasy in question, he is assaulted by a group of men on the street—rival men, that is.

So, how can we assure the neurotic that this woman could be nothing but his faithful companion if, by definition, she was chosen precisely because she corresponds to the statement "one fucks a woman"? The young man in question also tells himself a story—perhaps a bit less beautiful than those Anna Freud told herself—in which he is a spectator. He tells himself a story that excites him: he reaches orgasm. This is a fantasy in the full sense of the word. And yet, normally, we are in regression, or permutation; Anna's beautiful stories allow her to hide the fantasy of "a child being beaten," even if there is an identity of structure between the two. My analysand, on the other hand, ends up playing the role of the boy who is humiliated by his tormentor, confronted with his rivals.

Attraction and vertigo are one and the same thing for him. To ensure the logical integrity of the fantasy—namely, the Other with which he is confronted—he will need to respect the basic axiom that attracted him to her: "one fucks a woman." But if he accepts it, he is the one who will be betrayed, since she will also be the woman of others, of rivals. He is attracted by the object of the fantasy ($\$ \diamondsuit a$: a symbol corresponding to daydreaming), but faced with this object, he is himself excluded. The fantasy thus reserves the place of the voyeur for the neurotic who is subjected to it ($a \rightarrow \$$). To paraphrase Anna Freud, the daydream where the girlfriend fucks with others is interrupted by the blows of her tormentors, revealing a masochistic fantasy. In a certain way, the subject's position here is characterized by an imaginary capture where the woman being fucked "delights in being watched"—this is where the subject is involved. He is reduced to the voyeur, captured by a gaze that makes him enjoy (in every sense of the term). Thus, one can say that the object a—scopic and yet invisible—is hidden in the fantasy, giving it the function of an axiom:

But, on the other hand, this fiction connotes a relationship of enjoyment. We will call it so concerning the non-sexual relationship. This is how ($\$<>a$) should be read. It is the relationship of enjoyment. The fantasy as an axiom, as a formula,

writes this relationship of enjoyment, a relationship of enjoyment that is a relationship with the object a.[26]

The neurotic recoils from paying the high price of his anxiety, of making the
Other capable of receiving his libidinal reserve, a reserve incompatible with the
object of desire (the woman embodying the fantasized feminine enjoyment). The
neurotic would even prefer to fight with other men before giving up on this point of
jouissance; this is where he recoils. Notice that the same fantasy could support the
desire of someone else without the slightest symptomatic suffering. So, sometimes
he loves her (the fucked woman), and sometimes he despises her; the "accordion"
effect of the fantasy plays out fully during long periods that exhaust our hero (and
his partner). That the neurotic does not want to give up his anxiety means that he
does not want to give up his fantasized enjoyment because both are nothing more
than two sides of the same coin. Thus, even if his demand may seem paradoxical
(wanting to have his cake and eat it too), on the contrary, it abides by an implacable
logic. The neurotic's demand of wanting to have his cake and eat it too is precisely
what Lacan writes as "$\$<>D$": the subject divided precisely by the demand, and left
open to the drive (which I will return to).

What is important here? We have already mentioned the back-and-forth
described by Lacan in his seminar on anxiety, these steps forward and backward
that traverse this flexible and inextensible chain of subjection to one's fantasy. This
back-and-forth can only be imaginary, and it remains the place of passage (*poros*)
between the symbolic that one is subjected to and the real that escapes them each
time they traverse the drive circuit. Why speak of a "place of passage"? Upon
reflection, we can suppose that, revisiting his initial structuralism and the binarism that defines the subject on the basis of a simple opposition of two signifiers
("simple" here meaning indivisible), Lacan introduces an operation of reflexivity
that while it might go unnoticed under the slogan "the signifier is what represents
the subject for another signifier" is indeed operative. If we consider that this formula contains only two terms—namely, the opposition of two signifiers—we are
in a first stratum of Lacanian theory. If, on the contrary, we consider that this formula implies three terms, we are in what can be called Lacan's hyperstructuralism,
which implies reflexivity, or the possibility of changing places. Thus, Jean-Claude
Milner specifies, "It is, in my opinion, about conferring to the relation of opposition
(which is the only relevant relation in the structuralism of linguists) the property
of reflexivity.[27]" In *Anxiety*, Lacan already introduces variations into his different
schemas (notably the Z schema), which proves that he takes more liberties regarding a certain rigidity of structure. This simultaneity of rigidity and flexibility is
made possible through the articulations around the notion of fantasy, as he points
out in the *Ecrits*:

> What analytic experience attests to is that castration is what regulates desire,
> in both the normal and abnormal cases. Providing it oscillates by alternating
> between $\$$ and *a* in fantasy, castration makes of fantasy a chain that is both

supple and inextensible by which the fixation of objects cathexis, which can hardly go beyond certain natural limits, takes on the transcendental function of ensuring the jouissance of the Other that passes this chain on to me in the Law.[28]

The quotation shows, of course, the influence of Sade's work, but, additionally, it already proves that fantasy is indeed the "place of passage" between the "first Lacanian classicism" and the second classicism, where signifying binarism is questioned by the clinic itself. In other words, signifying discontinuity is shaped by a continuity that operates through the imaginary means of the fantasy structure. This is indeed an apt summarization of Lacan's almost descriptive phrase: "castration makes the fantasy this flexible and inextensible chain at the same time." This flexibility of the imaginary is typical of fantasy, in unison with the ego, while it is the inextensibility proper to the structure that makes the symbolic a defensive wall against the non-symbolizable real.

The fantasy thus indeed corresponds to this possibility of passage from a first to a second Lacan, with all the consequences that this implies in analytic theory. Let us again quote the following lines from *Anxiety*:

I may have been quicker in my discourse this morning than I had intended. Also, you see there indicated that there may be a possibility of passage, but this possibility can only be explored by going back, to that place where the imaginary castration functions to properly constitute, in its full right, what is called the castration complex.

I have already suggested that Lacan took a long detour to introduce the lack, or -ϕ, the non-specularizable dimension of the object that corresponds to the drive as autistic and unsharable. It is clear that this drive involves an impossibility in the sense that no object can completely satisfy it. Faced with this impasse of the impossible, implied by the symbolic and a real that is non-symbolizable, Lacan finds himself facing the theoretical necessity of introducing the uncanny—what is essentially imaginary—in the examples given by Freud and by the psychoanalytic clinic. This passage will be made through the "castration complex," which allows for "the study of the phenomenology of anxiety." What do I mean by this? That Lacan rediscovers, beginning with the seminar *The Object Relation*, the possibility of permutation.

Permutation and Mutation of Jouissance

Here I will deal with one last decisive inflection point in Lacan's thought. This inflection point involves the passage from a sort of fixity of the definition of the unconscious to something else, another definition that involves two modes of relation to the lack in the Other. There are two modes of back-and-forth as a response to this impossible that is -ϕ: the unconscious as production and the real as non-symbolizable. The fact that this led to a theory of fantasy is only a logical continuation within Lacan's work. Indeed, the change—which is almost one of paradigm—dates, I maintain, to his seminar *The Object Relation* and continues in the following year's seminar with the re-elaboration of the concept of the ego ideal. This conceptual change is then taken up later, both in the seminar on anxiety and in the one on the theory of discourses and even in his seminar *Encore*, which I have already mentioned. What may seem strange, as we have seen, is that in this last seminar Lacan relates the "change of discourse" (in the sense of passing from one discourse to another) to love.

Consequences of Permutation

What are the consequences of this change? Why is permutation supposed to bring about something "new"? I use this word deliberately because, as some may know, it was used by J.-A. Miller in his introductory lessons to the seminar The Formations of the Unconscious in 1998 in Barcelona; his small book containing the lectures is titled ". . . something new!" What does this seminar bring about that is new? The answer is unequivocal: it is the notion of ego ideal.

Indeed, the ego ideal is officially introduced in *The Formations of the Unconscious*, but it had already been conceived as such in *The Object Relation*, where Lacan introduces the notion of permutation and evokes, on several occasions, the ego ideal. Let's return to this tipping point at which a being, passing from desired to desiring, brings forth love, according to Lacan's formula. We might return again to Lacan's formula from *Encore*: "love is a sign of a change of discourse." What can this possibly mean? Since he speaks of discourse, it is only appropriate to refer this idea to his theory of discourses. Drawing on the board the four discourses, he separates them into two "groups": the hysteric's discourse and the master's discourse on one side and the university discourse and the analyst's discourse on the other. Lacan then specifies that the master's discourse "is illuminated by regression from" the hysteric's discourse. Similarly, the university discourse is illuminated by its "progress" toward the analyst's discourse. The words "regression" and "progress" only highlight a topological quarter-turn, a turn that refers to positions. Let's continue reading Lacan:

> In applying these categories, which are themselves structured only by the existence of the psychoanalytic discourse, one must listen carefully to the testing of this truth that there is the emergence of the analytic discourse at each crossing from one discourse to another: I say nothing else by saying that love is the sign that one changes discourse.

In other words, each time one passes from any one discourse to another, the analytic discourse emerges. This emergence constitutes a sign of love, as demonstrated by the appearance of one of its many forms: transference.

By reading between the lines, one can understand that this is a kind of passage from "beloved to lover." Thus, the "metaphor of love" is the minimal operator that would account for all subjective changes. For example, the "regressive" passage from the hysterical discourse to the master's discourse (the discourse of the unconscious) is a sign of love. In what sense? Let's take, for example, what Lacan calls "the first step of psychoanalysis"—namely, the maneuver made by Freud in the case of Dora when she puts him "up against the wall," summarized by this sentence: "Now that I've told you what's wrong, what do you want me to do about it?" Freud somehow rules in her favor and writes, "It is enough to turn her reproaches against the person who utters them."

Dora recognizes that indeed, she did everything to bring Mrs. K. and her father together—she facilitated their meetings. According to Lacan, if this is the first step in the history of psychoanalysis, it is because Freud obtained a "subjective rectification" from Dora. Here, according to the statement in *Encore*, the analytical discourse is at work. Dora recognizes herself as desiring in the sense that her desire is involved precisely there where she was complaining of being wronged, all the while being the "beloved" or desired object of Mr. K. This indicates that the transference is already operative. If this is the case, then love is too, because these two terms are co-extensive.

From this moment, we have the functioning of the analyst's desire and the transference inherent to it. Dora passes, mutates from one discourse (the hysterical discourse) to another (the master's discourse, that is, the discourse of the unconscious). It matters little that she remains, for a long time, in the hysterical discourse, that is, the discourse in which knowledge is produced for the Other in order to show him his impotence. What seems decisive is that during this brief moment of subjective rectification—a moment significant enough for Lacan to designate it as the first step in the history of psychoanalysis—Dora acknowledges the unconscious, the signifiers that determine her. She shows herself to be divided regarding her own complaint, which is characteristic of demand ($\$\diamond D$): yes, she is accusing her father; yes, she did everything so that he would meet Mrs. K.

There is a mutation here: one becomes the lover of a certain knowledge (first metaphor of love), a knowledge that the analyst embodies as desiring—desiring something other than an object of desire (second metaphor of love). Let us again recall Lacan's statement that "there is the emergence of the analytic discourse at each crossing from one discourse to another: I say nothing else by saying that love is the sign that one changes discourse."

We can summarize what can be deduced from Lacan's position with the following points: 1) each time there is a passage from one discourse to another, the analytic discourse is operative (p. 16 of *Encore*); 2) each time there is a passage from one discourse to another, there is transference; 3) transference is equivalent to love and therefore; 4) each time there is a passage from one discourse to another, there is love (= "sign of love").

Conclusion

The notion of permutation is a key paradigm in Lacan's work, but it is also useful in everyday clinical practice. Permutation implies a certain mutation of jouissance, if by jouissance we mean the ways of relating and subjectifying desire and the law, as well as mediating the other. Yet permutation also maintains a close relationship with the notion of fantasy, which allows for, on the one hand, the living being's attachment to a trait of the other through which they are represented, and, on the other hand, an avoidance of the signifier via the fantasy setup (let's recall the example of the man whose fantasy partner allows him to access a form of voyeurism), the passage à l'acte, and acting out.

Notes

1 Freud S., "A child is being beaten", in *The Revised Standard Edition of the Complete Psychological Works of Sigmund Freud*, Volume XVIII, Revised édition, translated by James Strachey and Mark Solms, Rowman & Littlefield, London, 2024.

2 Freud S., "A child is being beaten", in *The Revised Standard Edition of the Complete Psychological Works of Sigmund Freud*, Volume XVIII, Revised édition, translated by James Strachey and Mark Solms, Rowman & Littlefield, London, 2024, p. 175.

3 Freud S., "A child is being beaten", in *The Revised Standard Edition of the Complete Psychological Works of Sigmund Freud*, Volume XVIII, Revised édition, translated by James Strachey and Mark Solms, Rowman & Littlefield, London, 2024, p. 176.

4 Freud S., "A child is being beaten", in *The Revised Standard Edition of the Complete Psychological Works of Sigmund Freud*, Volume XVIII, Revised édition, translated by James Strachey and Mark Solms, Rowman & Littlefield, London, 2024, p. 177.

5 Freud S., "A child is being beaten", in *The Revised Standard Edition of the Complete Psychological Works of Sigmund Freud*, Volume XVIII, Revised édition, translated by James Strachey and Mark Solms, Rowman & Littlefield, London, 2024, p. 180.

6 Freud S., "A child is being beaten", in *The Revised Standard Edition of the Complete Psychological Works of Sigmund Freud*, Volume XVIII, Revised édition, translated by James Strachey and Mark Solms, Rowman & Littlefield, London, 2024, p. 181.

7 Freud A., *The Writings of Anna Freud. Volume 1: Beating Fantasies and Daydreams*, International Universities Press, Madison, 1974, p. 137–157.

8 Cambon F., *La conférence d'Anna Freud du 31 mai 1922, Les Lettres de la SPF, 2010/2 (N°24)*, éd. Campagne Première, p. 191.

9 Freud S., "A child is being beaten", in *The Revised Standard Edition of the Complete Psychological Works of Sigmund Freud*, Volume XVIII, Revised édition, translated by James Strachey and Mark Solms, Rowman & Littlefield, London, 2024, p. 185.

10 Freud A., *The Writings of Anna Freud. Volume 1: Beating Fantasies and Daydreams*, International Universities Press, Madison, 1974, p. 139.

11 Freud A., *The Writings of Anna Freud. Volume 1: Beating Fantasies and Daydreams*, International Universities Press, Madison, 1974, p. 142.

12 Freud A., *The Writings of Anna Freud. Volume 1: Beating Fantasies and Daydreams*, International Universities Press, Madison, 1974, p. 142.

13 Freud A., *The Writings of Anna Freud. Volume 1: Beating Fantasies and Daydreams*, International Universities Press, Madison, 1974, p. 149.

14 Freud A., *The Writings of Anna Freud. Volume 1: Beating Fantasies and Daydreams*, International Universities Press, Madison, 1974, p. 152.

15 Lacan J., "Presentation on Transference", in *Ecrits*, W. W. Norton & Company, 2006, p. 181.

16 Cottet S., *Freud et le désir du psychanalyste*, Seuil, Paris, 1996.

17 Freud S., "Remarks on dream interpretation", in *The Revised Standard Edition of the Complete Psychological Works of Sigmund Freud*, Volume XIX, Revised édition, translated by James Strachey and Mark Solms, Rowman & Littlefield, London, 2024, p. 101.

18 Freud S., "Remarks on dream interpretation", in *The Revised Standard Edition of the Complete Psychological Works of Sigmund Freud*, Volume XIX, Revised édition, translated by James Strachey and Mark Solms, Rowman & Littlefield, London, 2024, p. 108.

19 Freud A., *The Writings of Anna Freud. Volume 1: Beating Fantasies and Daydreams*, International Universities Press, Madison, 1974, p. 157.

20 Freud S., "Group psychology and the analysis of the ego", in *The Revised Standard Edition of the Complete Psychological Works of Sigmund Freud*, Volume XVIII, Revised édition, translated by James Strachey and Mark Solms, Rowman & Littlefield, London, 2024, p. 98.

21 Lacan J., *Anxiety: The Seminar of Jacques Lacan, Book X*, Polity Press, Malden, 2014, p. 117.

22 Lacan J., *The Four Fundamental Concepts of Psycho-Analysis*, Routledge, 2004, p. 68.

23 Lacan J., *The Four Fundamental Concepts of Psycho-Analysis*, Routledge, 2004, p. 75.

24 Lacan J., *The Four Fundamental Concepts of Psycho-Analysis*, Routledge, 2004, p. 103.

25 Lacan J., *On Feminine Sexuality the Limits of Love and Knowledge: The Seminar of Jacques Lacan, Book XX Encore*, Norton, New York, 1998, p. 16.

26 Miller J.-A., *Du symptôme au fantasme et retour*, unpublished lecture, 18 May 1983.

27 Milner J.-C., Personal communication.

28 Lacan J., "The mirror stage as formative of the I function", in *Ecrits*, W. W. Norton & Company, 2006, p. 700.

Chapter 5

The Desire of the Analyst

The notion of the analyst's desire is an original concept in Lacan's work. It is, in a way, the ethical correlate of the function of the object a. The analyst's desire should not be confused with the desire of the individual or with "unconscious" desire, in the sense of a desire whose existence has been previously concealed by the ego and the subject's fantasized relationship with others—a desire that the subject has been alerted to only through personal analysis.

The analyst's desire, rather, implies the bracketing of one's own desire and the activation of a desire that Lacan describes as a desire for "pure difference" (or even "differentiality"), where one object is no more valuable than another. In other words, it is this true indifference toward the object that will allow the analyst to operate, or to extract—and in the surgical sense—one signifying fragment rather than another. But that's not all. Lacan's idea is even more radical in the sense that for him, the analyst not only extracts (from the patient's history, for example) one signifier from a set of signifiers but also, through the handling of object a, attempts to rectify the analysand's subjective position (I use the word "rectify" here to mean a gamble and not a univocal action aimed at changing something in advance).

For the analysand's initial subjective position has compelled them to situate themselves in reference to an ideal called the "ego ideal": that vantage point from which they believe they see themselves from the Other, thereby granting the Other an ideal image. But this reality is not the same from the point of view of the other (ego ideal) as it is according to the unconscious desire that involves a as the object of all objects and the operation of the analyst's desire. We therefore have the ego ideal on the one hand, and the analyst on the other, understood as the one who somehow embodies the object a by the mere fact of seeking to rectify the subject in relation to their ideal. These are the two terms at play in Lacan's conception of the analyst's desire.

Separating the I from the a

In his seminar entitled *The Four Fundamental Concepts of Psychoanalysis,* Lacan explicitly develops his concept of the analyst's desire and provides an explanation of the direction of the treatment based on the object a, establishing the function

DOI: 10.4324/9781003614203-5

of the analyst's desire as what best corresponds to it. Lacan says that through this function, the analyst must separate, or keep "at the greatest distance," the ego ideal and the object a—the I from the (a): "Now, as everyone knows, it was by distinguishing itself from hypnosis that analysis became established. For the fundamental mainspring of the analytic operation is the maintenance of the distance between the I—identification—and the *a*.'"

Let us clarify the nature of the I being discussed here. We might recall that the ego ideal, noted as "I," is the psychoanalytic concept Freud constructs in *The Ego and the Id* and *Group Psychology and the Analysis of the Ego*, and it corresponds to what Lacan translates as the "unary trait" (*Einziger zug*). In what follows, I further develop my analysis of this concept by looking at Lacan's other formulations of the ego ideal as well as J.-A. Miller's elaborations on the "insignia.²'"

Freud's Diagram

One could argue that the ego ideal, as we are attempting to present it here, was somehow invented or reinvented by Lacan (even though it is present in Freud, the Lacanian definition constitutes an invention). On the other hand, what is not invented by Lacan is the notion of the unary trait, which is indeed from Freud. We can begin to clarify things by explicating the notion of the ego ideal from Freud's considerations in *Group Psychology and the Analysis of the Ego*. What is the unary trait in Freud? Freud's idea is to argue that the relationship of the ego to the object (or to another ego) is determined by an object (which we can call a signifier) or, more precisely, a representative trait of this object that functions as an ideal. Freud therefore takes the leader of the crowd as an example of a unary trait, an ego ideal that functions for a group. Let's tackle the diagram constructed by Freud that appears in chapter VII of *Group Psychology and the Analysis of the Ego*:³

How should we read Freud's graph? First, by distinguishing the ego, which is related to an object based on an identification that far exceeds this object. This means that the ego is just one of the elements of the unconscious that is most

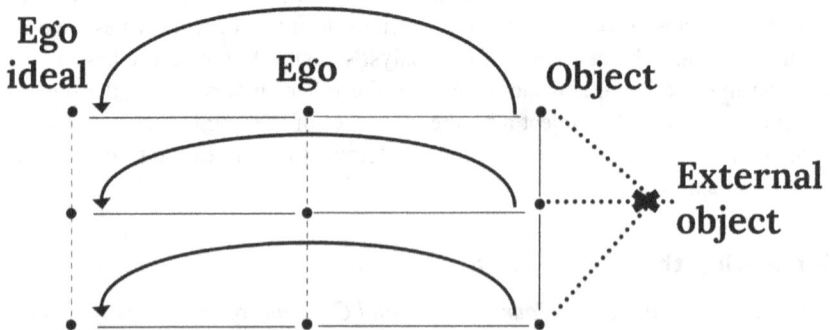

Figure 5.1 Group psychology.

connected to reality, almost seamlessly, as I have already indicated. This ego is related to a narcissistic object, or an object of desire, but only through the mediation of another object (or signifier) with which one identifies in the sense that they will see reality and its objects from the point of view of unconscious desire. We call this third object the ego ideal. In some sense, the ego ideal is the focal point of the thesis I develop in this book, if one considers that its hidden correlate is the object a.

If we take up the data deployed in the previous chapters, we should recognize that this ego ideal is what the subject turns to when confronted with an object (its own image or that of others) in order to obtain an authentication or assent, to see if it is desirable and what it is worth. In short: the ego ideal is reality. It is again in *Group Psychology and the Analysis of the Ego*, the very text in which he draws the schema above, that Freud isolates this third term—the ego ideal, or what one turns toward by identifying with it—as an example of one of three types of possible identifications. As I explained in the previous chapter, Freud's paradigmatic clinical example of what Lacan calls symbolic identification is the case of Dora.

Freud stipulates that what she identifies with can very well be a trait of the other, of the third element in the schema whose assent matters just as much. She identifies, that is to say, with a signifier much more than an object in its entirety. The fact that it is a trait of the object (the third object, toward which she turns) and not the object itself here is what allows psychoanalysis to be separated from a discipline that would otherwise function only through plausibility. For the true (*vrai*) is not the plausible (*vraisemblable*), and it therefore remains to be demonstrated as such.

Here is the example provided by the same Freud about Dora: she identifies with her father through a symptom, namely the cough—"Dora imitated her father's cough." Indeed, this is not plausible: what "identification" relationship can there be between the 18-year-old girl and the mustached, cigar-smoking father? Well, plausibility doesn't matter, for it is true that Dora adopts her father's point of view. She does so in order to be in relation to an object of desire (Mr. K.), as well as to the drive object (Mrs. K.) and the "oral" object that is involved in Dora's secret relationship with her. We must not forget that Mrs. K. is also a character in Dora's reality, a character who, although occupying a subsidiary place in relation to Mr. K., her husband, is no less important according to Dora's supposed libidinal economy.

We must continue our commentary of Freud's schema in order to fully grasp the role of the ego ideal. For if the relationship of the ego to the object of its desire is conditioned by the presence of a symbolic instance (the ego ideal) to which one identifies unknowingly, what hides this symbolic identification is indeed the existence of another decisive object (drive-related), an object akin to Mrs. K. in Dora's story. We know that Freud uses the leader as an example of identification with this ego ideal because what applies to a crowd also applies to a person and vice versa—the leader would be the ego ideal. So far, we have almost exhausted Freud's schema, except for one object, what Freud calls the external object, which he places almost outside his schema (via the dotted lines).

It is interesting to refer to the Freudian text *Group Psychology and the Analysis of the Ego* to read the relationship established between the idealization of an object and the state of being in love:

> The tendency which falsifies judgement in this respect is that of *idealization*. But now it is easier for us to find our bearings. We see that the object is being treated in the same way as our own ego, so that when we are in love a considerable amount of narcissistic libido overflows on to the object.2 It is even obvious, in many forms of love choice, that the object serves as a substitute for some unattained ego ideal of our own. We love it on account of the perfections which we have striven to reach for our own ego, and which we should now like to procure in this roundabout way as a means of satisfying our narcissism.[4]

Further, regarding the state of being properly in love, which resembles a state in which suggestion prevails—and even generalized suggestion, as in the case of a crowd hypnotized by its leader—Freud writes, "The whole situation can be completely summarized in a formula: *The object has been put in the place of the ego ideal.*[5]"

We know that Lacan makes much of this change of place not only in relation to idealization but especially concerning the analytic cure as such. Freud, for his part, differentiates identification as such (with an object)—where the ego acts as if it were itself the object with which it identifies, even defying what Freud calls "reality testing"—from the state of being in love—where, on the contrary, the ego makes the loved object coincide with the ego ideal, so that the lover finds themselves vulnerable, fragile, and at the mercy of the object they love. Even though Freud believes there is a difference between the state of being in love and collective suggestion (suggestion), he enriches the comparison by stipulating that,

> after the preceding discussions we are quite in a position to give the formula for the libidinal constitution of groups, or at least of such groups as we have hitherto considered—namely, those that have a leader and have not been able by means of too much "organization" to acquire secondarily the characteristics of an individual. A primary group of this kind is a number of individuals who have put one and the same object in the place of their ego ideal and have consequently identified themselves with one another in their ego. This condition admits of graphic representation.[6]

It is as if Freud is really referring to the state of suggestion, which is the subject of his text, to account for what his schema explains. In other words, the state of suggestion (of the masses) is what we deal with every day unless we are in love—and here I mean the pathological state of being in love (as the philosopher Leo Strauss emphasizes, "love with a capital L, does not love").

If Freud's schema corresponded to the fury of his time that led to totalitarianism, we could say that today Freud's schema corresponds to what happens on social networks. Freud's schema today is Facebook. And what is it that character-izes this non-loving state, this state of suggestion and collective mental debility called "social cognition" (Freud speaks of the "gregarious spirit")? The fact that the idealized object (according to Freud's word) is elsewhere, outside. For Lacan, on the other hand, there is no difference between outside and inside, and this might in fact summarize all of Lacan's explanations of the "reversed bouquet" in the previous chapters. The famous "inner eight"[7] schema allows him to formalize this. This "external object" Freud speaks of—as external as Mrs. K. in the Dora case—is the one that contains "the object of all objects," the function object a, or a sort of agalma that is present in the other. It is all the more present because one does not see it as such (which explains Plato's choice when he describes it as a "hidden treasure").

What this graph teaches us is that these "ideals" are, in turn, assembled by an external object that makes the same object of desire exist for a majority. Naturally, this conception of the object of desire could be an anticipation of Lacan's "Hegelian–Kojèvian" formula that "man's desire is the desire of the Other," since we have seen that the ternary structure of desire involves three terms, not two. One desires according to an ideal, the I of the ideal being a unary trait identical for the masses. In his seminar on transference, Lacan reminds us that "what is true for a collective is also true for two people," to which we might add "and for a subject," while being warned that this subject is not one.

Identifications

Freud would argue that the unary trait is a point of identification, an essential type of identification that can decide many things, such as how one will subjectively process sexuation. The example given regarding Dora's case could easily support such a hypothesis. Here I will briefly recall the three types of identification Freud presents in *Group Psychology and the Analysis of the Ego.* The first type of iden-tification is a kind of "primary identification" (understood as being prior to any possible type of identification).

For this type of identification, curiously, Freud speaks of "identification with the father," which defines an identification prior to any other and without which no other identification would be possible. Freud could have privileged the hypoth-esis of identification with the mother—since she is, so to speak, the first object—but this first object is precisely, and by definition, repressed. Therefore, there is no chance that another object would emerge if this first one were not essentially repressed—so repressed that it is as if it did not even exist. Thus, the so-called pri-mary identification, as such, should be found elsewhere—namely, with the father, and it should coincide with Freud's *Fort-Da.*

On this subject, J.-A. Miller explains, in the course mentioned earlier on the insignia, how the cry becomes a signifier and, depending on the response it elicits from the Other, a call. The cry is therefore situated before the response, or the sig-nification of this cry. For Freud, it is this response from the Other that constitutes the desiring being as such (the little child with the spool who says "*Fort-Da*") and it is what becomes the condition for entering language. This idea should be related to the "three phases of the Oedipus complex" described by Lacan (*The Formations of the Unconscious*) as well as the descriptions of cognitive or experimental psychology (cf. Rochat's studies); there are very early stages or phases in development that already shape the child's psychic functioning, or their relationship to the symbolic, long before the incidence of Oedipus or anything else—let us also recall the first two complexes Lacan described in his text *Family Complexes*—weaning and intrusion—that operate long before Oedipus.

But there is a second mode of identification that interests us greatly: the identification with the unary trait, which Freud equates with the leader, on one hand, and, on the other hand, with the father (Lacan will also identify the unary trait with the father). This is obviously not the same "father" as in the first identification described above, but rather, the father as the one who is incorporated toward the end of Oedipus and his legacy—namely, the ego ideal.

Finally, there would be a third type of identification that Freud exemplifies as follows: a young girl in a boarding school receives a letter from her boyfriend in which he announces that he is going to leave her; the young girl falls ill, and, in turn, the other girls fall ill. This phenomenon results from a type of identification that operates on the imaginary level and has nothing to do with either primordial identification (*Fort-Da*) or the compass-like identification of desire established at the end of the Oedipus complex. At stake here is more of an identification by proxy, where what is striking is the subject's indifference to the object (i.e., the fact that all the girls who fall ill because their friend has been abandoned by her boyfriend do not know the boyfriend at all, and this is actually absolutely unnecessary).

Regarding the second mode of identification, let's note a sentence by Freud, taken up by Lacan in his seminar on transference, which, in my opinion, is the key sentence of this seminar, as it gives rise to the notion of the ego ideal through permutation: the identification has taken the place of the object-choice [the object for Dora would be the father], and the object-choice has regressed into identification. What is essential to understand here is that the ego ideal determines everything related to the assumption of sexuation. The ego ideal is defined in the seminar *The Four Fundamental Concepts of Psychoanalysis* as an ideal point from which the subject sees himself as seen by the Other, or "place somewhere in the Other, from which the Other sees me, in the form I like to be seen.[8]" which coincides perfectly with the famous reversal toward the ideal that was discussed earlier. The other here is the Other with a capital O, the Other of the signifier and not the other as fellow human being (*semblable*), which we would write with a lowercase a. This is precisely the question to be asked, as this Other is beyond the specular other, the *semblable*. Moreover, the relation to the little other is determined by this ideal relationship to the Other of the unconscious signifier, as shown by both Freud's graph and Lacan's Z schema.

Let's go back to Lacan's landmark sentence, taken from Freud's text: "Identification has taken the place of object-choice, and object-choice has regressed to identification." How can this formula guide us in the direction of the cure? What does Lacan do with this regression? How does he situate this ideal point in the cure? It is worth quoting a long paragraph from the seminar on transference because it clearly states, using the case of a patient in analysis, the ideal point that the analyst is called to embody at a certain moment in the cure:

> In concluding today, allow me speak to you about the case of a female patient. I would say that this patient takes more than just liberties with the rights, if not the duties, stemming from the marital bond. And when she has an affair, Lord knows she is able to take its consequences to the most extreme point of what a certain social limit—that of the respect she derives from her husband's position—commands her to respect. Let us say that she is someone who knows how to sustain and deploy the positions of her desire admirably. And believe you me, she was, over time, figured out how to maintain altogether intact—in her family, I mean with her husband and her amiable kids—a force filed of demands that is strictly centered on her own libidinal needs. . . . What was I for this patient for quite some time? . . . I was her ego-ideal, inasmuch as I was the ideal point at which order was maintained, and in a way that was all the more necessary since it was on this basis that all disorder was rendered possible. In short, it was essential at that point time that her analyst not be immoral. Had I been so tactless as to approve of any her excesses, the result would not, I suspect, have been pretty behold.[9]

Evidently, this ideal point is necessary at a certain moment in the analysis, but it cannot be prolonged forever—Lacan himself warns us against such an eternalization (one would be curious to know the continuation of this analysis). Thus, when he asserts that most cures stop at this point of identification, it is a way of saying that there is a tendency to eternalize this ego ideal, this identification, and that therefore, the analysis should not only go beyond but also against this identification. This means that one must know how to differentiate the narcissistic object, or the object of desire (i(a)), from the role this object plays in psychic determinism according to the ego ideal, here embodied by another (the analyst) who observes what the cunning Dora does with her sexual life. He does not approve (Lacan emphasizes), but neither does he disapprove. In a way, she is putting her analyst to the test.

The Cure

In this differentiation, Lacan introduces the notion of the analyst's desire. He thereby criticizes the idea of regression, especially one that would pretend to bypass the signifying chain: "The regression people foreground in analysis (temporal regression, no doubt, providing one specifies that it is to do with the time of remembering) concerns only the (oral, anal, etc.) signifiers of demand, and involves the corresponding drive only through them.[10]" As I have already emphasized, access to the drive is only possible through the signifier and, moreover, by passing through the signifiers of sexuation. This distinctly modifies the idea of regression as it is conceived by analysts, even today, as an attachment (and why not preverbal) to drive objects: oral, anal (they will even speak of "pre-Oedipal transference," etc.). It is true that, with the object a, Lacan addresses a register that does not belong to the signifier and is radically distinct from it, but the cure cannot grasp this object a without the signifier. The object a is also at the basis of the imaginary fantasy, and it is thus at the origin of the demand, even if it is not reducible to it. If we can only reach the drive through the signifier, then it would be an illusion for the analyst to respond to the demand, because it is supported by an object that escapes it and for which one can only respond at the level of unconscious desire:

> Whether it intends to frustrate or to gratify, any response to demand in analysis reduces transference to suggestion. There is a relation between transference and suggestion, as Freud discovered: transference is also a suggestion, but a suggestion that operates only from on the basis of the demand for love, which is not a demand based on any need.[11]

In other words, one asks for something that can never be concretely satisfied. It is clear that

> this demand is constituted as such only insofar as the subject is the subject of the signifier is what allows it to be misused by reducing it to the needs from which these signifiers have been borrowed—which is what psychoanalysts, as we see, do not fail to do.; that is what allows it to be measured by referring it to the needs from which these signifiers are borrowed, which psychoanalysts, as we can see, do not fail to do.[12]

Therefore, to respond to the demand is to go astray regarding the object of desire; this object is, in any case, caused by the drive object. This is why distinguishing between two objects of essentially different natures becomes the true ethical path of psychoanalysis. In this regard, Lacan writes,

> But identification with demand's omnipotent signifiers . . . must not be confused with identification with the object of the demand of love. The demand of love is also a regression, as Freud insists, when he makes it into the second form of identification, which he distinguished in his second topography when he wrote *Group Psychology and the Analysis of the Ego*. But it is another kind of regression.[13]

What does this mean? Why does Lacan maintain that this is not the same regression? Because, indeed, it is not the same regression conceived by Freud and other psychoanalysts; "identification with demand's omnipotent signifiers" (what the desirous person demands as the narcissistic object of desire that could relieve their suffering) has nothing to do with "with identification with the object of the demand of love."

We already dealt with this issue when we looked at how Dora's stories or Lacan's "young homosexual woman" were centered on the privileged signifier of the ego ideal. Let us not forget that Lacan also called this signifier the "master signifier," or S1, the basis upon which the other signifiers are ordered. It is a symbolic identification that, as Freud indicates, holds only by a single identifying trait (the cough, for example). Lacan applies what I have already emphasized regarding the relationship between progression and regression to Dora's case; in relation to a certain progression of Dora toward an object that could situate her as being herself a phallic object of desire (thus the so-called Mr. K.), the symptomatic claim (since it is sustained by identification via the symptom of the cough) of her father's love is indeed a regression—she moves from being to having. In the case of Dora, what ensured Freud's failure was the confusion between "identification with the all-powerful signifier of the demand" ("the narcissistic object of desire" i(a)) and "identification with the object of the demand for love" (I(A))—the only identification that mattered for Dora. It is clear that this second mode of identification distinguished by Freud in Group Psychology and the Analysis of the Ego—an atypical form of identification through the symptom that differs from the classical Oedipal prototype—is a mode of regression that has nothing to do with direct access to drive objects. It is a significant regression and not a real one.

Interpretation

Separating the I from the a for Lacan means something specific. For Dora, this implies separating the imaginary object of desire (Mr. K.) from a symbolic identification with the father through the signifier *Vermögen*, where the identificatory symptom of the cough would be the libidinal and phantasmatic proof. Let's situate this significant configuration within Lacan's famous graph of desire.

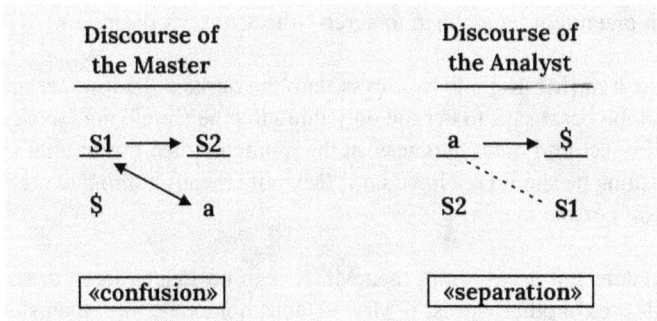

Figure 5.2 Master and Analyst Discourse.

We might take a shortcut here and say that "Mrs. K. is for her the embodiment of the question 'What is a woman?'" and therefore stipulate that the "a" in question is "Mrs. K." But let's not jump to conclusions. That Mrs. K. poses the question means it demands an answer, and Dora does not have that answer. This leads us to affirm that Mrs. K. is an enigma. Lacan indicates the following in this regard:

> This is why [Dora] resorts to all kinds of substitutes, the closest forms (. . .) she can find for this sign 'Φ'. If you follow Dora's operations, or those of any other hysteric, you will see that what is always involved is an intricate game by which she can, so to speak, complicate the situation by slipping φ, the lowercase *phi* designating the imaginary phallus, where it is needed.[14]

In Dora's case this manipulation comes in the form of a "Mr. K. is me." What does this mean? It implies that her way of answering involves the presence of Mr. K., and for what purpose? Lacan clarifies this point when he says, "Her father is impotent with Mrs. K.? Well, what difference does it make—she will serve as the copula herself. She will pay the price personally.[15]" And how will she "support it with her person"? Lacan continues,

> And since that is still not enough, she will into play the image—which takes her place, as I showed you a long time ago and demonstrated, of Mr. K. . . . For . . . Dora, or to any other hysteric, is to be the procurer of this sign in any imaginary form.[16]

In other words: she takes on the role of Mr. K. The imaginary answer ("she will do the copula") to the question "Who am I?" will be "I am Mr. K."

The Ego and the a

Mr. K. is thus necessary for Dora's identification. When faced with the question "Who am I?" the answer lies in the incarnation of the imaginary phallus in the form of an imaginary identification with Mr. K. And it is for this reason that when he says to Dora "My wife means nothing to me," according to Lacan's hypothesis— with which one might be inclined to agree—the artifice is disarmed:

> She casts him [Mr. K.] into the abyss, into the darkest shadows, at the moment at which the beast says to her the only thing that he should not have said whom she will reject into outer darkness, at the moment when this animal says to her the one thing he should not have said, "My wife means nothing to me." Namely, she doesn't excite me.[17]

And if she does not arouse him, then Mr. K. can no longer serve to support this image of desire. In other words, if Mrs. K. does not excite him, then she does not embody someone who knows "how to be a woman" and therefore, the imaginary, identificatory support that Mr. K. embodied for Dora inevitably vanishes.

What is essential is that Dora no longer has her imaginary support, and this is where she is left without an answer. To what? To sexuation (to sexual difference). This is why, even in the seminar on anxiety, Lacan associates the moment of anxiety in Dora with the desire of the Other—that is, with the fact that the signifier that could embody phallic jouissance is missing. In Dora's case, Lacan situates this moment of anxiety at the famous "scene by the lake," about which he writes,

> She always exchanges her desire [in her imaginary identifications] for this sign [namely, the phallus], we needn't look elsewhere for the reason for her so-called mythomania. There is one thing that she prefers to her own desire—she prefers to let her own desire go unsatisfied and have the Other hold the key to her mystery.[18]

For if the Other does not hold the key to the mystery of her desire, then there will be an unveiling—an almost delusional moment for Dora when she is confronted with the fact that Mrs. K. does not excite her traveling companion, Mr. K. (imaginary a or ideal Ego—*moi idéal*).

The a is the "substitute or metaphorical object [thus Mr. K.], for something that is hidden, namely minus phi, her own imaginary castration [not being, as a woman, the phallic object of the man's desire], in her relationship with the Other [namely, Mrs. K.]." It is clear that Mrs. K. occupies the place of the Other par excellence. Let's specify: the father occupies the place of the Other par excellence, and it is Mrs. K. who, after the "lake scene," comes to bar this Other. The phrase "my wife means nothing to me" makes this Other incomplete, showing it to be barred, even castrated. This is the castration with which Dora is confronted. Before that, we can suppose that she was asleep; the a as such did not emerge, and Dora would have easily found her place within Freud's schema from *Group Psychology and the Analysis of the Ego*.

But if Mrs. K. embodies the object of anxiety and the question of the "desire of the Other" (let's remember the letter she writes to Dora, in which we find the famous phrase "if you want"—a true question addressed to everyone that concerns the question of desire, the desire for something else and thus a true "what do you want?"), then what is the object of the fantasy? It is Mrs. K. herself, of course, but is this in fact what Lacan tells us in his 1960 seminar? I'm not so sure. What do we call the object of the fantasy in this 1960 seminar on transference? Let's recall Lacan's anecdote about the young man and his little "sport car." Lacan says that the young man's races are addressed "to the girl"; whether she is real or imagined is of no matter, but she is certainly an imaginary in the sense that she might be entirely missing, which leads Lacan to say, "the girl can be altogether superfluous and need not even be present. In short, in this context, which is the one in which the ideal ego has just assumed its place in fantasy.[19]" Thus, the ego ideal (i(a)) is arranged from the (imaginary) fantasy which is determined—according to these pages from the seminar on transference—by an ideal point: the ego ideal, this ideal point where, in the fantasy, I see myself "as seen by another." The fantasy accommodates this ideal point which is the ego ideal:

> What is the ego-ideal? The ego-ideal, which is closely related to the play and function of the ideal ego, is truly constituted by the fact that at the outset, if he has his little sports car, it is because he is from a fine family, because he is a rich man's son. . . . [I]f Marie-Chantal, as you know, joins the Communist Party, it's to piss off her father.[20]

In other words, being against the father is, in a way, being identified with him. To give another example, we could take the case of an obsessional who, not wanting to be a merchant like his father who only thought about money, wanted to become instead an intellectual—that was his demand. A radical and yet simple misunderstanding was revealed to this obsessional when it was pointed out to him that in order to not have money, one doesn't have to become an intellectual. This is why Lacan can assert, "It is around the function of the ideal that the subject's relationship with external objects is arranged." In other words, all objects have a common characteristic—and this is the function of the unary trait.

The Analyst and the Hysteric

Lacan believed that the hysteric could teach the analyst something: namely, that he or she is indifferent to the object of desire. This is, in fact, the essence of the Socratic method, which, by allowing the dialogue to be carried by the dialectic of the signifier, has no pity for the object itself, as it is completely indifferent to it. Thus, it is the signifier that is differential, not the object. Lacan indicates that the analyst must follow the Socratic path:

> What Socrates knows, and what the analyst must at least glimpse, is that at the level of the little 'a' [that is, the semblable, to whom love is addressed], the question is entirely different from that of access to any ideal."

In other words, the object itself is completely indifferent, "and the analyst can only think that any object can fill it," because "there is no object that is more valuable than another—this is the mourning around which the analyst's desire is centered." This last sentence is fundamental and says everything one needs to know about what Lacan calls the function of the analyst's desire. Separating the I from the a means, in this seminar on transference, that the analyst says, when the other loves him— according to transference love—"You love me, but in the name of a certain ideal."

And yet, Lacan's reasoning becomes more complex. From the seminar *The Four Fundamental Concepts of Psychoanalysis* onward, the status of the object a changes. Around 1964, the object a is no longer the semblable. While before this date, it referred to the semblable and nothing else, from 1964 onwards, the object a becomes, so to speak, the true partner of the "I," of the ideal, or the unary trait, as

I explained it via Freud's schema and Lacan's analysis of it. Lacan could therefore say, "I love in you . . . in the name of a certain ideal . . . the object 'a,' which is my own flesh, the drive, and I mutilate you."

In this regard, it seems important to refer to an article by J.-A. Miller devoted to the "insignia[21]" that summarizes some lessons from his course on this theme. The psychoanalyst begins the article by returning to the master's discourse to remind us that it is primarily the discourse of the unconscious and that, for this very reason, "it is not made to validate [our] considerations on the insignia." Why this statement? What appears as the primary given and defines the master's discourse in Lacanian algebra is the fact that it is a discourse that leaves aside the object a. The object a must remain outside the signifying articulation (just as it is outside Freud's schema), and this is why it occupies the place of the real. In other words, it occupies this place because it is non-symbolizable—that is, it is not represented in the signifier.

According to Miller, the signifier seems to confiscate the representation of the subject because it can only be referred to another signifier, and not to an object. The Lacanian subject is an empty set, and psychoanalysis, in a certain way, cultivates the relevance of this empty set. This means that, on one hand, we have the S1/S2, where the living being is almost confiscated, since it is represented indirectly, and on the other hand, a, which would come to make this incomplete being more present. Thus, what Lacan calls object a can in a certain way complete the subject, the subject who is emptied out because it is represented by the signifier.

J.-A. Miller argues that the subject divided by the signifier can be completed in three different ways: with "I", with "S1", and with "a". To put it differently, we can recall that the Lacanian subject (that is, the subject of desire) does not have a real referent, as it relies on the abolition of the referent. Faced with this lack of a referent, the subject has only two ways to exist: either he exists at the price of being represented by signifiers, and thereby loses something of the drive (no direct relationship with objects); or he positivizes this lack through the path of fantasy, but again loses what represents him since, in fantasy, he is passive and reduced to being an object in a kind of "calculated acting out" or ritual staging of an (illusory) abolition of loss. What loss? The loss he experiences due to not having a direct relationship to the Thing, and which makes him go through a pseudo-objectification of it, taking himself as an object and making himself appealing to the ego ideal, much like the massified idiot in *Psychology of the Masses and Analysis of the Ego*— Freud emphasizes the passive component of this kind of collective suggestion. Put another way, a subject can oscillate between the sacrifice of its ego to the other to whom they devote excessive love (the state of being in love in all its glory) and fantasy, in which they find contentment by indulging in it. Let's note that in this regard Freud believes that after sexual satisfaction (fantasy), the desiring person can be relieved of the oppressive weight of the idealized object of love, at least for a few moments.

Miller adds in *The Four Fundamental Concepts of Psychoanalysis* that identification with the ego ideal, or the point "from which the Other sees me in the form where it pleases me to be seen," is a representation, "a call to fill the void left by the loss" that is caused by a. But let's clarify: since this "loss" is a loss of the jouis-sance (enjoyment) of the Thing (I don't need to remind you that we do not have a direct relationship to anything due to signifying alienation), something needs to fill in for it. This is, according to Miller, what Lacan invented—"a filling-in that is not of the signifier."

Miller adds that, thanks to this, "there is not only the fulfillment of the ideal." Between the I (or S1) and the a, there is "alienation/separation"; "it is in the same place that S1 and small a are successively inscribed." It is therefore necessary to differentiate the identification fixed by the representation (the I) from the object a (which pertains to an identification before what we can call—at least, for now—its "being"). Miller thus raises the question of the relationship between the signifying representation starting from the unary trait and its "being of jouissance," embodied by the small object a, which is no longer the little other—no longer "Mr. K.," if you will.

But for there to be a relationship between the unary trait and the small a, we need only refer to the two discourses that Miller contrasts in the article I am ref-erencing here: the discourse of the master and its transition to the discourse of the analyst. Let's not forget that in this chapter we are exploring the notion of the analyst's desire—this mainly involves a change in the tightly bound articulation between I and object a. The author recalls that when Lacan addresses identification in Freud, he places both the object a and the I in a relationship of "conjunction, of confusion." And Miller adds, "The object a, however inassimilable it may be in the signifying order, is still susceptible to superimposition in the same place as an essential signifying marker, which is the capital I.[22]" Thus, while in the master's discourse, there is confusion between I and a, the analytical discourse, on the other hand, is characterized by the requirement of a separation between these two terms.

Miller explains this with regard to transference as it unfolds in the analytic cure: "it involves that the outcome of transference is identification insofar as the very economy of transference is based on suggestion." Here we have Lacan's

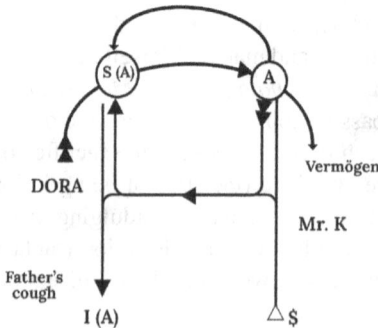

Figure 5.3 Graphe of desire.

first approach to transference: transference as a tendency toward suggestion. In this regard, I hypothesize that to conceive of transference as mere repetition and reduce interpretation to the interpretation of this transference ("you repeat with me the same thing as with your father," etc.) is a way of suturing the living by identification, and thus by suggestion. This is where the discourse of the analyst marks a difference from the discourse of the master, and this is how Miller finds a place for this key phrase from Lacan's seminar *The Four Fundamental Concepts of Psychoanalysis*:

> if transference is that which separates demand from the drive, the analyst's desire is that which brings it back. And in this way, I from the drive, diverts the demand . . . the desire of the analyst is what brings it back there [let's clarify: brings it back to the drive]. And in this way, it isolates the a, places it at the greatest possible distance from the I that he, the analyst, is called upon by the subject to embody.[23]

And what the analyst is called upon by the subject to engage in is indeed suggestion. Miller complements this idea by stating, "While transference brings the demand back to identification by diverting it from the drive, the desire of the analyst, operating in the great A, opens the path to the drive.[24]" He then points out that Lacan, in the *Écrits,* specifies something strange when the latter argues that, when the desire of the analyst opens the path to the drive, "the fantasy becomes the drive."

I wanted to arrive at this point to show, thanks to J.-A. Miller's commentary, that there are terms here that lend themselves to confusion in the various readings made about the graph. If we think of symbolic identification "I(A)," we will notice that the subject does not recognize themselves in their relationship to the drive, but in their relationship to the imaginary fantasy, which precisely has as its condition the hiding of the drive object. This is what makes Miller say that the only notation we have of the drive on the graph of desire is the one linked to the fantasy in "$\$ \diamond a$," whereas this formula does not show the drive object as such but only the imaginary object of the fantasy. And Miller adds, "This has continually deviated the reading of Lacan, because this object a is even more evident when it comes to the drive . . . it is precisely here [in the drive ($\$ \diamond D$)] that it would be legitimate to write ($\$ \diamond a$).[25]" This is valid if we think, for example, that the a in $\$ \diamond a$ deals with the drive object (one of the forms of the object a insofar as the drive object is "partial," without relation to the total, narcissistic object).

The Case of "The Man in the Raincoat"

The preceding pages suggest that Lacan's object a would be one of the names of the original castration of the living being (the notion of object a would arise insofar as it would be the subject's "being," lost by the operation of the signifier), provided that this castration were not reduced to its sole imaginary register.

Castration involves the body as fundamentally separated from a primal, pre-genital jouissance. This jouissance is thus impossible as such and reduced to a "surplus of jouissance" that is attached to the pleasure of phallicized erogenous zones—that is, put in relation to objects of desire.

But if the pleasure of the erogenous zones can cause displeasure, it is because one enjoys beyond pleasure, and why wouldn't it be so? The signifying body is separated from jouissance (Lacan sees here the only real castration that matters), but jouissance persists through the drive object. Castration and the object a are thus linked, so that drive objects are only a necessary consequence of the action of repression. The living being thus affected by symbolic castration oscillates between $(-\varphi,)$ a symbolized world of which the subject of the signifier is only an effect, and a, the drive object, in such a way that what is at stake is obtaining a certain articulation between the lowercase a and $(-\varphi)$—that is, the value of castration—where the desiring subject can qualify themselves as lacking and address the Other of the demand. These two elements—the $(-\varphi)$ and the drive a—are thus linked, showing that the unconscious, structured like a language, is in tension with an object that is not in language.

We will take as a starting point here one of Éric Laurent's reported clinical cases:[26] a man came to see an analyst because he had what he called "vice"; he was always choosing women who were already taken as his love objects, which forced him each time to compete with the wronged men. He always had ideas of attacking these men with knives; he had, in fact, a great passion for this. The rivalry with men had led him, at the time of taking the exams that would lead him to practice the same profession as his father, to experience bouts of vomiting, a situation incompatible with the position he was supposed to normally occupy.

During the analysis, a childhood scene is brought up: he reveals that, at the age of 9, he was seduced by an educator who was a family's friend. He found himself in a pastoral setting, in which there was an axe somewhere. This seduction—consisting of mutual masturbation—prompted in this man a response that manifested as a compulsion to wear something that had previously been unbearable to him: a plastic raincoat (the kind his mother used to insist he wear at the slightest hint of rain) in order to masturbate beneath this "cover." This practice had continued ever since and served as a universal remedy for all his worries, which is why he did not complain about this fantasy. As Laurent points out, this is a well-constructed fantasy, and one might then wonder how to reconstruct it with him in the treatment.

Let's see what the analysis of this case reveals. Everything seems to start with a dream, in which facing the intrusion of a gaze, the dreamer responds by defecating. The analysis of his relationship with cleanliness reveals a screen memory: around the age of 4 or 5, he surprises his mother (or sister, he's not sure) as she opens the bathroom curtain and appears naked. The patient notices the feminine castration, but in one corner, he perceives a plastic shower cap made of the same material as the raincoat. From this dream, the author notes a transferential phase characterized notably by manifest aggression. A debt to his analyst leads him to wonder why, during the session, he makes noise with some coins he has in his pocket. A song comes to mind in which a sailor does the same thing; the song ends with the debt being paid off with a stab.

This idea referred to the analyst is interpreted by the patient as a form of rivalry where he comes to see someone "to piss them off . . . to fill, as he does everywhere, the various raincoats he encounters in his life." The discovery "that he came to fill the Other with his being in this form" (with shit) causes him a very specific disturbance, prompting him to see a doctor: for about fifteen days following the session in question, he has the impression that his feces contain a white substance "as if it were semen." He is reassured by the doctors, who tell him that he is not ill. Laurent explains, "Here, we see how the transferential moment—stagnation after the first phase of subjective alienation in which he recovers the screen memory—this transference-stagnation is also the bet he makes . . . 'bet-object' that appears in the anal form.[27]"

Subsequently, each time he recalls the screen memory of the bathroom, he sees a knife in the scene—the same knife he always kept in his pocket in case of a fight. Another dream occurs during the therapy: he is at his aunt's house ("he sees in the dream all the details 'with the vividness and 'hallucinatory' precision of reality'"), and on the other side of the wall, he knows there are three women: his mother, his aunt, and his sister. He then begins to search through a trunk containing women's clothing—something that is forbidden—and when he pulls out his hand it is covered in blood. He himself carefully analyzes this dream to identify what corresponds to the memory of encountering castration. He discovers why he couldn't evoke the bathroom memory without the knife being involved:

this knife was the remnant, present in the form of the axe in the seduction scene, the remnant of the real traumatic scene, namely the discovery of castration in the woman (sister, mother); the discovery of the absence of a penis in the woman. The moment of the forbidden act (evoked in the therapy with the dream) of searching under the mother's skirt is necessary for an elaboration of this position.[28]

According to Laurent, three steps are to be retained of the relationship this subject maintains with the Other. First, there is his rivalry with the man (which corresponds to the idea of the knife always present in his pocket). Second,

in the transference, one separates what is in the pocket: on the one hand the knife, the axe, these signifiers with which he evokes $-\phi$, castration, and phallic value; on the other hand, the necessity of always having in the pocket the feces required to soil the raincoat screen that the Other presents to him.

Finally, after this "transferential ambivalence," the true significance of his rivalry with men emerges, as does the significance of the debasement of his love life, where he is always forcing a woman into action: "it is a way of constituting the partner as 'dregs'" He always finds "shitty partners" in life.

What interests me is the way Laurent presents the construction (or reconstruction) of the fantasy from the analysis; how do we construct it if it is already constructed from the beginning of the treatment? The equivalence "money = shit" is rather imaginary. However, what underlies the structure is a separation: "on the one hand, everything that comes from castration, and on the other, everything that depends on the object." In his fantasy, he oscillates between one extreme and another: on the one hand, the signifiers of castration; on the other, the object a, disguised as shit, which comes to relieve him of the signifiers of castration (knife, axe, naked woman). At the beginning, the fantasy of an Other (who appears when he masturbates under the "protective" plastic screen) "only unites and confuses the value of castration—which matters in relation to the Other—and the anal object, the stain he manages to make on the aforementioned screen." However, toward the end, these two objects are separated in such a way that the process of the treatment (this separation) is a way of assuming castration—a castration that operates a separation between the signifier that divides the subject and the object a that comes to relieve him of this loss. Initially, he managed to maintain

> the value represented—what he had discovered with the seduction of the educator—and the phallic value he had for his mother. This is why the raincoat—which was previously a source of discomfort and embarrassment when his mother wanted him to wear it—becomes afterward a remedy that attests to what he was for his mother, the phallus of his mother.[29]

In this treatment, Laurent writes, the strategy was to go beyond phallic semblance, a semblance that would give meaning to the sexual relationship by confusing the signifier and object a, or language, and drive. This "beyond is constituted by the object, which in this case is the anal object, through which he constitutes the Other analyst as well as the Other sexual: the woman of his thoughts." This means that the being of the desiring subject is made of this forbidden (forbidden because impossible) jouissance, which is phallic jouissance. More than a castration, it becomes a promise. This shows that real castration is the one that forever excludes the object a from the signified body. The fact remains that in a treatment, it is through language that one can grasp this drive object that escapes language. This is how an analytic treatment reaches a point of irreducibility that coincides with what can be called the drive, or with what are called erogenous rims, devoid of commensurate objects.

Notes

1 Lacan J., *The Four Fundamental Concepts of Psycho-Analysis*, Routledge, 2004, p. 273.
2 Miller J.-A., *Ce qui fait insigne, Unpublished Course (1986). We Can Read a Brief Summary in "Le sinthome, un mixte de symptôme et fantasme"*, No. 39, La Cause freudienne, Paris, 1998.
3 Freud S., *Group Psychology and the Analysis of the Ego: The Revised Standard Edition of the Complete Psychological Works of Sigmund Freud*, Volume XVIII, Revised

édition, translated by James Strachey and Mark Solms, Rowman & Littlefield, London, 2024.

4 Freud S., *Group Psychology and the Analysis of the Ego: The Revised Standard Edition of the Complete Psychological Works of Sigmund Freud*, Volume XVIII, Revised édition, translated by James Strachey and Mark Solms, Rowman & Littlefield, London, 2024, p. 104.

5 Freud S., *Group Psychology and the Analysis of the Ego: The Revised Standard Edition of the Complete Psychological Works of Sigmund Freud*, Volume XVIII, Revised édition, translated by James Strachey and Mark Solms, Rowman & Littlefield, London, 2024, p. 105.

6 Freud S., *Group Psychology and the Analysis of the Ego: The Revised Standard Edition of the Complete Psychological Works of Sigmund Freud*, Volume XVIII, Revised édition, translated by James Strachey and Mark Solms, Rowman & Littlefield, London, 2024, p. 107–108.

7 Lacan J., *The Four Fundamental Concepts of Psycho-Analysis*, Routledge, 2004, p. 271.

8 Lacan J., *The Four Fundamental Concepts of Psycho-Analysis*, Routledge, 2004, p. 268.

9 Lacan J., *Transference: The Seminar of Jacques Lacan, Book VIII*, edited by Jacques-Alain Miller, Cambridge, 2017, p. 341–342.

10 Lacan J., "The direction of the treatment and the principles of its power", in *Ecrits*, W. W. Norton & Company, 2006, p. 530.

11 Lacan J., "The direction of the treatment and the principles of its power", in *Ecrits*, W. W. Norton & Company, 2006, p. 530.

12 Lacan J., "The direction of the treatment and the principles of its power", in *Ecrits*, W. W. Norton & Company, 2006, p. 530.

13 Lacan J., "The direction of the treatment and the principles of its power", in *Ecrits*, W. W. Norton & Company, 2006, p. 530.

14 Lacan J., *Transference: The Seminar of Jacques Lacan, Book VIII*, edited by Jacques-Alain Miller, Cambridge, 2017, p. 245.

15 Lacan J., *Transference: The Seminar of Jacques Lacan, Book VIII*, edited by Jacques-Alain Miller, Cambridge, 2017, p. 245.

16 Lacan J., *Transference: The Seminar of Jacques Lacan, Book VIII*, edited by Jacques-Alain Miller, Cambridge, 2017, p. 245.

17 Lacan J., *Transference: The Seminar of Jacques Lacan, Book VIII*, edited by Jacques-Alain Miller, Cambridge, 2017, p. 245.

18 Lacan J., *Transference: The Seminar of Jacques Lacan, Book VIII*, edited by Jacques-Alain Miller, Cambridge, 2017, p. 245.

19 Lacan J., *Transference: The Seminar of Jacques Lacan, Book VIII*, edited by Jacques-Alain Miller, Cambridge, 2017, p. 340.

20 Lacan J., *Transference: The Seminar of Jacques Lacan, Book VIII*, edited by Jacques-Alain Miller, Cambridge, 2017, p. 340.

21 Miller J.-A., "Le sinthome, un mixte de symptôme et fantasme", *La Cause freudienne*, 39, 1998.

22 Miller J.-A., "Le sinthome, un mixte de symptôme et fantasme", *La Cause freudienne*, 39, 1998, p. 10.

23 Lacan J., *The Four Fundamental Concepts of Psycho-Analysis*, Routledge, 2004, p. 273.

24 Miller J.-A., "Le sinthome, un mixte de symptôme et fantasme", *La Cause freudienne*, 39, 1998, p. 10.

25 Miller, J.-A., "Le sinthome, un mixte de symptôme et fantasme", *La Cause freudienne*, 39, 1998, p. 10.

26 Laurent E., "El hombre del impermeable", in *Concepciones de la cura en psicoanalisis*, Manantial, Buenos Aires, 1984, p. 110–116.

27 Laurent E., "El hombre del impermeable", in *Concepciones de la cura en psicoanalisis*, Manantial, Buenos Aires, 1984, p. 114.
28 Laurent E., "El hombre del impermeable", in *Concepciones de la cura en psicoanalisis*, Manantial, Buenos Aires, 1984, p. 115.
29 Laurent E., "El hombre del impermeable", in *Concepciones de la cura en psicoanalisis*, Manantial, Buenos Aires, 1984, p. 115.

Chapter 6

The Gaze That Is Not Seen

In his seminar on anxiety, Lacan introduces "five forms of the object petit a." His radical discovery is that these five forms revolve around what he calls a "zero point"—what necessarily corresponds to any form of narcissistic object. This notion of the zero point seems essential to me, especially since it reappears in the discussions of the following year's seminar when one of the forms of the object a, to which I devote this chapter, is specified: namely, the gaze. Indeed, Lacan suggests, in the session of the seminar *The Four Fundamental Concepts of Psychoanalysis* titled "The Split of the Eye and the Gaze," this central idea:

> The gaze may contain in itself the *objet a* of the Lacanian algebra where the subject falls, and what specifies the scopic field and engenders the satisfaction proper to it is the fact, for structural reasons, the fall of the subject always remains unperceived, for it is reduced to zero. In so far as the gaze, *qua objet a*, may come to symbolize this central lack expressed in the phenomenon of castration, and in so far as it is an *objet a* reduce, of its nature, to a punctiform, evanescent function.[1]

The statement is somewhat enigmatic: what indeed should we understand by this idea that the gaze "generates the satisfaction proper to it"? Why does it differ from other types of satisfaction (for example, sexual satisfaction)? What does he mean by "the fall always remains unnoticed," and more precisely, what should we understand by "fall"? Beyond religious or metaphysical connotations, the fall, in Lacan, is linked to satisfaction; for example, concerning orgasm, one can read "As for orgasm, it bears an essential relation to the function we define as the falling-away of what is most real in the subject.[2]"

It is worth recalling that our author, after pronouncing the statement we just read, gives as an example of orgasm that which someone might experience in "hastily handing in the copy of a composition," which, it must be admitted, is a satisfaction proper to more than one. One more step and one might be tempted to think that the handed-in assignment would be a "punctiform, evanescent" satisfaction were it not for the possible bodily fluids that would render it anything but evanescent. Lacan's idea, then, is to maintain that just as Freud described auto-eroticism as a mouth that

DOI: 10.4324/9781003614203-6

might say, "Too bad I can't kiss myself," similarly, scopic pleasure is only made of the repeated and always failed attempt of the eye to see itself, which ultimately isolates a "cause of desire" that is rather "asexual.³"

In any case, according to Lacan's idea, the gaze would appeal to a form of pleasure whose orgasmic fall is "reduced to zero," so that the phenomenon of castration would not translate into a threat but rather into a particular form of pleasure for the body that experiences it. This separation (because it is "punctiform, evanescent"?) is the equivalent of a fall, something of which the desiring subject is deprived. But precisely because of the particularity of the object involved in satisfaction (sight)—an object that cannot be confused with the object precisely being looked at—this deprivation is not "torn" from the body. It is noteworthy that something similar can be said about the oral drive, which does not confuse itself with any particular food even if the clinical form of force-feeding might make us think that we are far from deprivation (the opposite example, that of anorexia, shows us that the object of satisfaction is almost indifferent).

Just as in a film, there is a moment that can be called the reversal, so too in an essay, we reach a similar point. In these pages, it is through the reversal operated by the notion of the gaze in Lacan that we reach a kind of theoretical reversal. The psychoanalyst's idea about the gaze can be condensed by these few lines:

> In the scopic field, everything is articulated between two terms that act in an antinomic way—on the side of things, there is the gaze, that is to say, things look at me, *and yet I see them*. This is how one should understand those words, so strongly stressed, in the Gospel, *They have eyes that they might not see*. That they might see what? Precisely, that things are looking at them.⁴

I have emphasized the phrase "and yet I see them" to make tangible the fact that, for the subject as conceived by Lacan, vision is already a kind of denial, a refusal of the gaze; through vision, one does not recognize that one is being looked at constantly. The subject is convinced that it is he who sees, as in Lacan's optical diagrams or those of the cognitivists, but in truth, it is the gaze of the other that is primary.

From the outset—from birth—vision is there to refuse the gaze of the other as a gaze, as it is a gaze by which one is primarily an object, rather than a subject. Just as consciousness (and with it the ego) represses the unconscious, vision represses the fact that the gaze is and always has been primary, even at the phenomenological level. Examples abound, such as the patient who says, "it was by closing my eyes that I felt looked at" or the little child who at the very moment the train enters a tunnel, making the space dark, exclaims, "look, we can't see anything!" (which means, "Things (or objects), they are watching us.") We can also think of nighttime fears that are always linked to the lack of light, when vision is extinguished and it is the gaze (of things) that threatens the desiring subject. There is also, of course, the children's game of hide-and-seek, where the pleasure mixed with anxiety is not so much about being discovered but rather about evading the gaze (hence the importance of preserved places, hiding spots that children can always find in care settings).

And yet we could hold a similar line of argument about the voice given that babbling is primary and that children speak their first words without knowing what they are saying. Speech is learned first, and only much later does one learn to read and write; this means that one didn't know what one was talking about and couldn't connect what was said to a fixed referent (which is the origin of language misunderstandings due to things that are "heard but not understood" in childhood, as Freud wrote). Note that in the autistic child, who has become for us a sort of negative image of socialized desire mediated by the other (just as Freud saw neurosis as the negative of perversion), the sequence is exactly reversed: the child learns to read and even write before speaking. Thus, the spoken word is primary and preexists the named thing, if we think that the latter is nothing other than the named thing from the other, which one finds (or not) in the world. Thus, the voice is primary, and the name of the thing comes later (which is why in his graph of desire, Lacan writes "voice" in a vector that, in a second phase, becomes a signifier).

But what seems equally crucial in this approach to the gaze and vision is that the "split," the *Spaltung*, of the eye and the gaze is homologous to the *Spaltung* of the subject and the unconscious. It is homologous to the famous *Ichspaltung* that Freud spoke of, which Lacan took up from the beginning of his seminars; as an example, he formulated that the graph of desire represents the *Spaltung*[5] inherent to the speaking being, that is, the subject discovered by Freud. To put it briefly, just as the ego has a function of misrecognition concerning unconscious determinism, so too does vision allow one to scotomize what causes the act of seeing beyond any perceptual need. Thus, the relationship between vision and the gaze—in which they almost oppose one another—goes even further to be equivalent to the relationship that opposes the ego to the subject.

If vision is confused with a direct apprehension of the world and, thereby, with the function of consciousness, it is also the corollary to a consciousness that believes itself to be transparent to itself—the corollary to a consciousness that perceives itself as consciousness in the manner of the Cartesian *cogito* and all the phenomenology that follows. Vision is the corollary of consciousness; Lacan could not have said it better. It is enough to take a slight interest in artificial intelligence and observe how, in experiments with brain–computer interfaces, mere eye movement (eye-tracking) is enough to trigger a response from the device.[6] In these experiments, the device is a continuation of vision as a source of misunderstanding, the misunderstanding that claims that vision is primary and that the device and everything else merely follow the user's initiatives. But this is not the case because the device itself is already an obstacle (a gaze) to the intentions of the subject, so that the "command initiative" is a mixture that comes as much from the user's initiatives as from the program's initiatives.

The Gaze and the Cogito

We might also be familiar with Lacan's analysis of the Cartesian *cogito*, particularly present in his seminar *The Four Fundamental Concepts of Psychoanalysis*. Lacan aims to highlight the "punctual and evanescent" nature of the *cogito* as a suspension of all acquired knowledge, in the manner of the subject of science.[7] And what is this subject of science if not the suspension of the ego and its attributes through the consciousness that thinks itself? For it is methodological doubt that prevails over egoic knowledge.

In response to "I think, therefore I am," we have two possible attitudes: either it is a sort of denial of discontinuity, of the *Spaltung* to which I just alluded through the illusion of the primacy of consciousness, or, on the contrary, it affirms discontinuity by promoting methodological doubt, independently of consciousness. If vision is the primordial correlate of consciousness and the subject promoted as an autonomous being, the very nature of the unconscious is, on the contrary, "non-autonomous." We begin to understand why Lacan introduces a split between vision (correlate of consciousness) and something else—the gaze as the presence of the unconscious, as the non-autonomy of the desiring subject, or an irreducible exteriority.

The gaze thus conceived implies realities that escape any egoic apprehension. Lacan aptly emphasizes that we should not claim that certain objects are invasive in psychosis; rather, it is their very structure that renders them unsuitable for egoization.[8] In other words, there is something that is not simply reduced to a "gaze seen" by me but is, on the contrary, something in the Other that appears as nonassimilable, similar to what we tried to pinpoint with the phenomenon of anxiety. Lacan himself indicates this, in 1964, with these words:

> The gaze sees itself—to be precise, the gaze of which Sartre speaks, the gaze that surprises me and reduces me to shame, since this is the feeling he regards as the most dominant. The gaze I encounter—you can find this in Sartre's own writing—is, not a seen gaze, but a gaze imagined by me in the field of the Other.[9]

What is crucial in this quotation and in the emphasized word is that I have rendered imaginary something that, in the Other, constitutes a stain. After all, as I have already mentioned before, in the setup of the optical schema, it is precisely the gaze of the other as such—this gaze that leads me to a meaning and a misunderstanding—that I repress or scotomize. This is the gaze whose significance I fail to recognize as the source of my own meaning, starting with the image of my body. And this is also why Lacan believes that the gaze itself, in the scopic exchange with the other, is evanescent:

> What is involved in the triumph of assuming the image of one's body in the mirror is the most evanescent of objects, since it only appears there in the margins: the exchange of gazes, which is manifest in the fact that the child turns back toward the person who is assisting the child in some way, if only by being present during the game.[10]

It is clear that in the 1960s, Lacan was preoccupied with this question of sharing with the other, we must, however, understand this as a form of sharing that is misunderstood as such—that is to say, it is not what is shared that is in question (the body, the little car) but rather what causes the sharing. After all, there is no reason why there should be a sharing of desire with the other.

Merleau-Ponty, or rather, Lacan's Merleau-Ponty, would have pushed this phenomenology, whose foundations are laid in *Phenomenology of Perception*, to its limits. If Merleau-Ponty's work explored what we might call "the regulatory function of form" (namely, the predominance of the gestalt in perceptual experience), through which being exercises itself to make the "double" of representation practiced by idealism from Plato to Kant's transcendental aesthetics coincide, his posthumous work *The Visible and the Invisible* takes "the next step by pushing the limits of this very phenomenology."

How does Merleau-Ponty accomplish what Lacan designates as the next step, by which he frees himself from phenomenology? The question seems important to me because Lacan refers to it to introduce the famous split between the eye and the gaze. He describes a kind of reversal in the philosopher's work, a reversal he wanted to articulate precisely through a critical reading of *Phenomenology of Perception*, published in the journal *Les Temps Modernes* in homage to Merleau-Ponty.[11] The critique consists in showing that what is determinative in the perceptual act is indeed the gestalt that precedes the individual, a precedence that presents itself in the form of the gaze.

In other words, the desiring subject is anticipated by the gaze, which is "everywhere" and thus nowhere; this nowhere is the very scotoma against which vision stumbles; vision will necessarily be delayed relative to the gaze, which is posited as primary and is supposed to cause it. Here's a vacation-themed example: in the blue sky above a beach, a helicopter suddenly appears. The vacationers look at it, see it, but it goes without saying that it is the machine that imposes itself first and attracts the gaze (the vision) of the onlookers; it is the vacationers who are being watched by the machine. But one can also try to find examples in everyday life. We look at women on the street, but why not think that it is rather those dressed as women who watch and trigger the vision of men and also of other women? We would thereby better understand Lacan's idea that women embody the phallus, rather than lack the phallus. One could thus say that we are not aware of (we do not see) women.

The Gaze as Instrument

What is this gaze? It is not simply the fact that someone is looking at us; the gaze is not reduced to the act of looking or being looked at, which, for Lacan, is nothing other than the misappropriation of the gaze as he attempts to promote it. The eye, as such, is merely a metaphor for what he tries to convey about the split of the subject. What matters to him is what he calls "the thrust of the seer," which is indeed prior to the act of seeing and, by that very fact, causes vision as the desire for something. To draw a parallel, one could use Lacan's remark that people who are deaf-mute from birth can hallucinate voices; here too, the voice preexists perception as such, since the individual does not hear and has never heard.

This notion of preexistence seems important to me insofar as it allows us to understand another notion that at times seems somewhat elusive in Lacan's work, the notion of the instrument. One could say that the word "instrument" serves as an instrument for Lacan to account for a certain reversal carried out by psychoanalysis—by Freud, and by Lacan, I would say—whereby the subject is dislodged from its status, erected by the philosophies of consciousness, as a transcendental subject, overarching and encompassing the world through thought. It is also not enough to simply assert that there is an "unconscious," as the term is so overused that it might be granted a univocal meaning. Rather, the notion of the unconscious affirms that, for psychoanalysis, the individual is not autonomous; they are permanently preceded by language or by the desire of the other, conditioned by the other.

This individual does not have a manual—not because the manual does not exist, but because they are merely the instrument of it. If, through the notion of the object a—of the gaze as being present everywhere but especially invisible as such—Lacan reduces the subject to being merely an effect, then we will see that this function of a is equivalent to that of an instrument through which I am objectified: "Hence it comes about that the gaze is the instrument through which light is embodied.[12]" This illuminating idea, that light takes form through what looks at me and makes me a "photographed object," highlights quite well the reversal of the cogito as a subject of consciousness (which would, in turn, be different from the "punctual and evanescent" cogito, an effect and not a cause of representations). To assert, therefore, that the subject "is a tableau" and not a spectator of the tableau reveals the reversal performed by Lacan through this kind of substance that is the object a.

If Lacan uses the example of the tableau by asking, "What is a tableau?," it is because it is the privileged artifice of consciousness (or of representation). In chapter IX of *The Four Fundamental Concepts of Psychoanalysis*, he draws two triangles nested inversely, where the apex of one triangle touches the base at the median of the other and vice versa, to indicate that one corresponds to the "subject of representation" and the other to the gaze. The idea represented here can be translated as follows: the triangle representing the subject of representation is that of the subject of consciousness, while the other triangle corresponds to the gaze—that is, the subject of the unconscious. The subject of representation will take the tableau being looked at as a representation, precisely where

I assure myself that I know quite a lot about it, I assure myself as a consciousness that knows that it is only representation, and that there is, beyond, the thing, the thing itself (. . .) In my opinion, it is not in this dialectic between the surface and that which is beyond that things are suspended. For my part, I set out from the fact that there is something that establishes a fracture, a bi-partition, a splitting of the being to which the being accommodates itself, even in the natural world.[13]

These statements seem fundamental to me. Why? Because Lacan is saying that a painting is not what ordinary people imagine it to be. The painting is not made to be "seen" (or looked at); the painting, instead, looks at the one standing in front of it: "It is in this way that the painting does not play in the field of representation. Its purpose and effect lie elsewhere." The subject of the unconscious, as instrumental-ized by the object a—whether by libido or by the lamella—shows that this new concept of Lacan's is the most original of his work; it is radical insofar as it intends to give a "made in Lacan" stamp to his reading of Freud and psychoanalytic ethics.

It is also well-known that Lacan is interested in Holbein's painting *The Ambas-sadors*, where, by way of anamorphosis, a more or less indistinct figure, depend-ing on the spectator's position, becomes a skull. I will not dwell on this question here, but one might also mention Michael Fried's book *Absorption and Theatri-cality*,[14] where the author proposes the primacy of absorption (which he also calls anti-theatricality, insofar as the painting does not assume the spectator's vision), particularly in the context of Chardin or Greuze's paintings. Through the theory of absorption (where the gaze of painted characters is absorbed by something other than the painter who paints them and, therefore, by the supposed place of the spec-tator), the painter renders uncertain the exchange of gazes between the characters and the one observing them. The gaze directed elsewhere only highlights that the gaze is primary and that the vision (of the spectator) can only follow. This negation of the spectator can also be understood as a refusal of vision, and even a refusal of eye contact between the characters and the spectator, such that the reciprocity between vision and gaze tends to be nullified (to the detriment of vision), empha-sizing the function of the gaze. The paintings Fried describes thus tend to accentu-ate the split between vision and gaze.

The Seer's Shoot

What does Lacan mean by the "push of the seer" (which incidentally reminds us of the "push towards the woman")? What could be the significance of recalling here a potential relationship between the two? In my view, there is only one reason, which is to point here to a sort of "becoming"—becoming what one is not, that is, lack. More precisely, why does Lacan name this instance independent of the eye as such, this instance that causes the gaze, or this "something before the eye"? Let us remember that this is the same author who conceived of the "optical schema" where, precisely, we have a concave mirror before the eye, a mirror that presents this Other who is always there. I have addressed this at length in the previous pages. I have also assumed that the gaze of the other as such is repressed (forgot-ten) in the alienation of seeing, where we stick to the visualized objects as if they were mere objects we contemplate.

The cause of vision is not the object being viewed but rather what pushes one to see; this place of sharing with the Other cannot help but convey lack because it is a form of sharing. This indirect and alienated relationship with the Other, which empties objects of their substance by transforming them into a mere pretext for what pushes one to see, reflects what is repressed in the Other (its being) and can only be found through its mediation.

The desiring subject will seek what is most intimate elsewhere, in an intimacy that precedes them. Just as the signifier precedes the being's arrival into the world, so too is the gaze already there, anticipating any possibility of vision. Therefore, things must be situated as follows: the gaze precedes the act of seeing, which is why there can only be an imaginary reciprocity between seeing and being seen, between looking and being looked at. Or, to put it differently, the reciprocity between looking and being looked at corresponds to a second period, which establishes itself as a kind of repression of the first period where "in my existence, I am looked at from all sides.[15]"

That the gaze precedes the act of seeing is indeed what Lacan indicates, just as cognitive theories forty years after him also do, as I have shown previously, but we can go even further. When the psychoanalyst believes that the oral and anal drive objects correspond to the field of demand and that the other objects he has identified—the gaze and the voice—belong to the field of desire, which is by definition nonshareable, we are very likely returning to the famous optical schema of yesteryear in the sense that the gaze anticipates vision (concave mirror) and the voice precedes speech (the word that also anticipates desire because it is nothing but pure misunderstanding without a real referent). In fact, the book could end on this observation. In any case, it is important to understand this: the objects of demand (oral and anal) do not help us understand the object a. Only the objects of desire can account for—albeit with a certain opacity—what this Lacanian discovery is about. The opacity is also to be taken literally for the gaze object is also not ideally positioned to easily grasp the object a; in the field of visual perception, everything is constructed so that the perceiving subject considers themselves a subject of perception (percipiens) and not as a perceived object (perceptum). In fact, the object a as such stains the epistemè and its transmission.

That being said, it goes without saying that we see. We are even condemned to vision: "this seeing to which I am subjected in an original way," declares Lacan. In other words, we have no choice but to see, which is paradigmatic of what he calls "our relationship to things . . . ordered in the figures of representation." In this notion of our relationship to things, we find the object relation. Lacan, for his part, refrained from using this formulation, dear to analysts of the time (like Maurice Bouvet), not because of a rejection of the existence of a relationship to objects—for this relationship is indeed effective—but rather on the principle that there exists a primitive and true relationship to a total object in harmony with the living.

On the other hand, in *The Object Relation*, Lacan mainly introduces the primacy of the symbolic, which is in some way a negative relationship to the object since it destroys it as a positive reference by stripping it of all positivity. The object is determined by the symbolic register and not by an immediate relationship, what would be a correlate of the imaginary register and supposedly determined by a primary relationship to the object. What the theory of the object a adds to this initial state of affairs—namely the preexistence of the symbolic—is what escapes the symbolic as such, and likely causes it. The object a is essentially partial, not total. After all, why not think of the symbolic itself as nothing more than a repression of "objects a" that determine and anticipate the living? In Lacan's formulation ("this seeing to which I am subjected in an original way") one also sees a trace of a primary relationship to things; this would be more primal, original, and primitive relationship to a sort of "ontological reversal, the foundations of which would be found in a more primitive institution of form.[16]" It is this institution of form that constitutes the driving force of vision, this "something before the eye" that pushes one to see.

"I Saw Myself Seeing Myself"

Let's pick up where Lacan locates the split between the eye and the gaze, in what he perceives as the very foundations of consciousness. He recalls the beginnings of psychoanalysis when Freud situates what he calls the "primary process"; this primary process will be located in relation to the id—namely, to the unconscious as such, or the unconscious that does not access representation and which, in a way, is "as if it did not exist." This timeless unconscious, which does not know the principle of contradiction and which Freud calls the "other scene," manifests itself precisely in the form of a rupture with consciousness, in another space—"another scene, between perception and consciousness.[17]"

Let's return to our starting point because it is essential to understand the conception of the gaze as a non-specularizable object in Lacan: when the child turns to glimpse the real objects reflected in the mirror, they can perceive everything except their own body. Their own body becomes a necessary scotoma because it can only be perceived in the mirror. The body cannot perceive itself, and certainly, the eye cannot see itself. The parallel is striking with the Cartesian cogito insofar as it can no longer think itself and has value only as a performative subject: "[which subject] I defined last year as punctual and vanishing: that relationship to knowledge which, since its historically inaugural moment, has retained the name 'cogito.'[18]" It is surprising that Lacan uses the same adjectives to describe both the subject (of the unconscious) and the gaze as object a.

In the seminar *The Four Fundamental Concepts of Psychoanalysis,* Lacan cites a poem by Paul Valéry, *La jeune parque,* where one can read, "I saw myself seeing myself." For him, this is a precise example of the individual's misrecognition, of consciousness's misrecognition, objectified by the gaze. This corresponds, the psychoanalyst thinks, to the Cartesian cogito, where the subject grasps itself as thought. This is why Lacan can insinuate that there is a (seemingly self-evident) function of misrecognition here: the misrecognition of consciousness as being without a body, and of vision as eliding the gaze. Wryly, Lacan suggests that if one says, "I warm myself by warming myself,[19]" given that there is a reference to the body, the aspect of "self-grasping" seems less obvious; the body does not obstruct but, in any case, interposes itself in the activity of warming oneself (up). Therefore, one can see that Lacan, with his notion of the gaze object (object a), almost intends to found a new "transcendental aesthetic," as he specifies in the seminar *Anxiety*, which presents itself as a sort of research laboratory. In Freudian experience, neither intuition nor transparency is available to the subject; no intuition of consciousness can be considered originative, and thus it cannot serve as the foundation for any transcendental aesthetic.

The Dream: The Royal Road to Object a

We are all aware that Lacan begins his return to Freud through several readings of Freud—one of which, famously, is the analysis of the dream of "Irma's injection.[20]" And no one is unaware that Freud stipulated that the dream was the "royal road" to the revelation of the unconscious. What matters in the dream of Irma's injection, as in the case of the dream "Father, can't you see that I'm burning?" is the function of awakening, with the exception that, because it is Freud—filled as he was with an ambition and a desire to go beyond what is received, a desire for knowledge— he does not wake up. Nevertheless, even if he does not wake up—and especially because he does not wake up—there is a function of awakening in the stain (and why not write the task) of the dream where the throat of this patient literally looks at the dreamer.

Again, we are faced with the fact that the dream, before "seeing," "shows"—as has been indicated to highlight what stands out—what stains a dream and in some way objectifies the dreamer, placing them back in their role as a spectator (provided one sees that the spectator is passive in the face of the gaze). We can see how, through the imaginary, something like a double of the living being appears in the form of the gaze-object—the viewing subject is arrested, subjected to an object that is irreducible to them. In this way, both the gaze and the voice are those "reals" that allow us to grasp the unconscious as such in the sense that the subject (with their consciousness, their customary identifications) is reduced to a sort of residue—more effect than cause—of the unconscious. Much of Freud's work is concerned with this aspect of the gaze as the umbilicus of the unconscious, both in *The Interpretation of Dreams* and in his text on anxiety, *The Uncanny.* And one could also revisit Lévi-Strauss's discovery, which I commented on by reconnecting it to the object a-gaze—"What is this red beast?"—as the address of the all-seeing world to the subject who seeks to respond to it with the signifier.

Conclusion

The voice and the gaze, more than the other examples of object a, would be two "objects that cause desire" ("*objets cause du désir*") in the sense that they introduce us to human desire while differentiating themselves from consciousness, identified by Lacan with the senses of vision or hearing. According to the psychoanalyst, object a is "prior to the constitution of the status of the common, communicable, socialized object."

It is certainly not by chance that in the optical schemas I have presented throughout the previous chapters, two functions seem to determine the relationship to the world or —and this amounts to the same thing—the very birth of being in the world: vision (which is sustained only by the gaze of the other, and which in this sense can only precede the living being) and hearing (correlate of the voice) as what hears the world, this world that is named by the other. It is the other who decides the name and function of the object "table," for example. A wooden table is more than just wood; it is above all a socialized form, a gestalt. Yet who does not remember the faces inscribed in the wood, the pareidolias that our perception reconstructs after a first moment of surprise in the moment when the wood looks back at us? After all, this must be quite similar to the moment of awakening that I just previously described. Voice and gaze can be obstacles to any representation: it is no accident that the example of the gaze object is best understood in front of the mirror (as what looks and not as what serves vision) and the voice object in the presence of the echo, where our own speech becomes audible.

I should also say a word about the gaze-object and sexuation. It is related to the latter, but obviously preexists it. Sexuation, as Lacan conceives it, especially in his seminar *Encore,* is a choice of the speaking being—a choice tinged with contingency, to which object a naturally lends itself. But if object a is upstream of the choice of sexuation, then it forces us to separate it from the latter in the sense that no genealogy can be traced between the drive object and sexuation. The latter is distinguished from object a whether gaze or voice.

Vision is the condition of "social cognition" (imitation, learning, etc.); to put it simply, it is the foundation of everything. But this cognition, which psychoanalysis calls the symbolic, is only achieved at the cost of the greatest misunderstanding ("referential opacity"): that the world and its things must be erased by naming them. But the things are there, with their own reality, well before our knowledge, and they continue to look at us, even if we see them over and over again to better master them. In some respects, the gaze becomes the unconscious as such—against which vision can only be its repression—insofar as it objectifies the living being by rendering it an object.

Notes

1 Lacan J., *The Four Fundamental Concepts of Psycho-Analysis,* Routledge, 2004, p. 76–77.
2 Lacan J., *Anxiety: The Seminar of Jacques Lacan, Book X,* Polity Press, Malden, 2014, p. 168.
3 "What did Lacan put in place of bisexuality? He put exactly the opposite. He put nullisexuality. When he brings the object *a* into the fantasy, it is precisely the object *a* insofar as it is asexual.", Miller J.-A., *Du symptôme au fantasme et retour,* unpublished lecture, 24 November 1982.
4 Lacan J., *The Four Fundamental Concepts of Psycho-Analysis,* Routledge, 2004, p. 109.
5 Lacan J., *Formations of the Unconscious: The Seminar of Jacques Lacan,* Polity Press, 2020, p. 321.
6 Kosmina N. and Lecuyer A., "A conceptual space for EEG-based brain-computer interfaces", *PLoS One, 14*(1), 2019.
7 Gueroult M., *Descartes, selon l'ordre des raisons. Volume 1: L'âme et Dieu,* Aubier, Paris, 1968.

8 Lacan J., *Anxiety: The Seminar of Jacques Lacan, Book X*, Polity Press, Malden, 2014, p. 120.
9 Lacan J., *The Four Fundamental Concepts of Psycho-Analysis*, Routledge, 2004, p. 84.
10 Lacan J., "On my antecedents", in *Ecrits*, W. W. Norton & Company, 2006, p. 56.
11 Lacan J., "Hommage à Merleau-Ponty", in *Autres écrits*, Seuil, Paris, 2001.
12 Lacan J., *The Four Fundamental Concepts of Psycho-Analysis*, Routledge, 2004, p. 106.
13 Lacan J., *The Four Fundamental Concepts of Psycho-Analysis*, Routledge, 2004, p. 106.
14 Fried M., *The Book Absorption and Theatricality: Painting and Beholder in the Age of Diderot*, University of Chicago Press, Chicago, 1976.
15 Lacan J., *The Four Fundamental Concepts of Psycho-Analysis*, Routledge, 2004, p. 72.
16 Lacan J., *The Four Fundamental Concepts of Psycho-Analysis*, Routledge, 2004, p. 72.
17 Lacan J., *The Four Fundamental Concepts of Psycho-Analysis*, Routledge, 2004, p. 56.
18 Lacan J., "Science and truth", in *Ecrits*, W. W. Norton & Company, 2006, p. 728.
19 Lacan J., *The Four Fundamental Concepts of Psycho-Analysis*, Routledge, 2004, p. 80.
20 Lacan J., *The Ego in Freud's Theory and in the Technique of Psychoanalysis, 1954–1955, Book II*, W. W. Norton & Co, 1991, Chapter XIII.

Chapter 7

The Commodity and the Object a

It is fashionable to assert that Marx was ahead of Freud in that he supposedly introduced a novel conception of fetishism in the sense that the word, which originally
described the phenomenon of transferring a soul onto an object or, more precisely,
establishing a psychological relationship with an inanimate being—here we refer
to the original description of the concept of fetishism as introduced by Ch. de
Brosses in anthropology—becomes applicable to other objects. By doing so, Marx
extends the scope of the concept far beyond its original use, thereby altering its
nature. We see that something of the idea of mana, which I have already discussed,
continues to haunt the research. It is clear that the term undergoes some modifications in its use by Marx and Freud for the very simple reason that even if the white
observer might be somewhat astonished by the animistic behavior of the primitive
man, it is not certain that he considered this behavior abnormal since it belonged to
an otherness (that of the primitive man).

For the white observer, it is essential to maintain an objective, scientific, and
experimental distance; not being part of the tribe and not believing in the fetish,
one can position oneself in a laboratory-like situation. But what about the use of the
term by Marx and Freud? The latter also conceived of the fetishistic patient as an
animist insofar as he represents a pathological case. But this is not where Freud's
change lies: the change or mutation consists in going much further and finding that,
in some cases, it is the relationship to the partner that is fetishized, as the latter is
entirely subjected to an erotic trait that renders him desirable to the fetishist. This
is why Freud is interested in Alfred Binet's text on love and fetishism,[1] two fields
that belong together insofar as in both, a particular part of the other's body becomes
essential—essential in an exclusive way. Freud universalizes the fetishized relationship to the other. Should we therefore stop at exceptional cases? Are we not
describing sexuality as being essentially fetishistic since there is no direct relationship with the partner? This conceptual shift must be taken into account.

And what about the shift made by Marx? Does he not also universalize the
fetishistic relationship to commodities?[2] Does he not perform a true Copernican
inversion by establishing that exchange value takes precedence over use value? If
we assume that exchange value is to the signifier what use value is to need, is there
not a crushing of use value by exchange value, with the latter becoming a total

DOI: 10.4324/9781003614203-7

social fact (Mauss)? Is the buyer not anticipated by the exchange value, even if they benefit from the use of commodities? If this latter hypothesis is relevant, then the correlation between the "fetishistic character" of the commodity, as described by Marx in the first book of *Capital*, and sexuality, which can be conceived as a kind of extended sexual fetishism, contains the new keys to all relationships with objects in the modern world, insofar as the relationship to the object allows for the fulfillment of libido and pleasure in living beings.

It may seem surprising to use the notion of fetishism to understand what governs the modern economy, reducing it to a kind of generalized fetishism. One might see a paradox in reinjecting an animistic relationship into objects in societies where this relationship is supposed to be foreclosed. We know that this is not the case and that a society is never entirely within the domain of science without retaining the operationality of other registers (animism, totemism).[3] The discovery of animism should also be able to be confirmed in any civilization, even those affected by modern science, as Marx and Freud have show.

Let us return, then, to the shift produced within the very notion of fetishism, a shift that would require slightly modifying the definition of the phenomenon. A. Iacono, who has looked into the question of fetishism by making a brief history of it, concludes that there is a sort of "epistemological break"[4] between the original use of the word fetishism, attributed to de Brosses, and its modern use, attributed to Marx and Freud. For him, the break concerns the change in the observer's point of view: the white observer describes a fetishistic phenomenon "from the outside" since he is not part of the tribe, whereas the theorists, affected by science, do so "from the inside" by describing a phenomenon that occurs in their own societies. But upon closer examination, isn't it at this level that a difference must be marked between the anthropological use of the term and the use made by Marx and Freud? Is it really a break?

Both Freud and Marx produce knowledge, knowledge that must disregard the opinion of the observer. Marx and Freud align themselves with the Newtonian dictum *hypotheses non fingo*, just like President de Brosses. In our view, it is one and the same perspective—that of the subject of science. Thus, it is not in the same way as Iacono that we will speak of a break. An entirely different question arises, due to the fact that within the concept of fetishism as used by Marx and Freud, there is a kind of necessary mutation for its development. If the animistic phenomenon is true for the ethnological case, then it must be found in all societies. It is, therefore, about extending the phenomenon far beyond the local fact described by de Brosses to a total social fact.

Inverted Animism

If we return to our analysis of Lévi-Strauss's reading of mana, we will be obliged to understand that the ethnologist also generalizes a notion that was normally reserved for certain unknown objects (such as a particular animal or object) to extend it to the concept of a "floating signifier," through which the signifier *mana* is nothing other than the name of what has no name (like *machin, truc, bidule* in French). But that is not all: the idea is to argue that every signifier behaves in this way. For Lévi-Strauss, there is an excess of signifier over the signified, just as one could argue that there is an excess of exchange value over use value. And if exchange values are "exchanged" among themselves through the intermediary of men, one might almost be tempted to assert that there is a kind of inverted animism, whereby the living entities (with a soul) are the men, and the system of exchange (as a total social fact) studies us with a certain objectivity.

If, in Lacan, the object a is the gaze (rather than the reverse—I'll allow myself this conjecture)–then man is an object objectified by this gaze. One need only recall Lacan's considerations about the dream and the "it shows" to see to what extent the subject is objectified and thus an effect of what happens elsewhere to determine him. We should thus proceed with a cascade of conceptual inversions: 1) fetishism is a kind of animism whereby a soul is transferred onto an object; 2) because we are subjected to objects, we must transfer a soul to them (thus an inversion by generalizing a hypothesis, because the nature of the concept changes: we have an "animistic" relationship with objects, but we do not know it); 3) 2 obliges us to derive another consequence, which is that the desirer can only be subjected, both to objects and to signifiers (besides, if 2 is true, it is because objects are no longer merely objects but rather signifiers that function in a network). With 3, we witness yet another inversion, one that announces the end of objects and the primacy of the symbolic system, and we would thus have the theoretical foundation for the positions of Freud (if we accept the equivalence "sexuality = fetishism"), of Marx (every commodity is only valuable in relation to another commodity, regardless of the buyer), and of Lévi-Strauss (mana is not just a useful signifier, but it is the very example of the functioning of language as a total social system; it is the signifier of signifiers).

What remains is the object a that we are studying in this text. It claims to be what escapes the signifier, but it escapes it in the sense of having a life of its own, a potential source of anxiety, which reminds us of *mana*; Lévi-Strauss reminds us that in French, for example, we say *machin* to name something we do not know very well because *machin* is related to *machine*—something that operates on its own, independently of our will, and whose functioning is mysterious (let us also recall the automata evoked by Freud in *The Uncanny*). Thus, one could say that there is some *machin* or *machine* in every object despite the fact that the signifier is there to name it and give it a place in our lives. *Machin, truc,* and *bidule* are the signifiers that cover up what *machines* by itself with what makes us anxious. *Machin, truc, bidule* are the signifiers that attempt to name the object a inherent in any signifier functioning as such. The gaze determines and precedes being to the extent that this gaze, which is everywhere, would reduce the beings subjected to it—beings who are nonetheless endowed with a soul—to the status of mere objects caught in the net of the signifier or in the net of exchange value.

Fetishism thus conceived describes a reversal of the individual's relationship with their objects, particularly because they find themselves in a relationship of subjugation to these objects. There where they believed they were the master on board, they were in reality subjected and, paradoxically, even became objects themselves (this latter point should be seen as not a cause but rather a consequence of the reversal). Therefore, if there is an epistemological break in the use of the concept of fetishism, it corresponds to an extension of the phenomenon of fetishization rather than to a change in the observer's point of view. Put more clearly, 1) the concept of fetishism described by de Brosses only concerns certain objects to which an animistic cult is devoted; 2) the commodity fetishism derives its meaning only from the "commodity form" and not from matter, which governs the function of all commodities from the moment that only their form defines them; 3) similarly, sexual fetishism, in this context, is only of interest insofar as the fetishistic function is extended to all sexuality—libido can only be satisfied by the form of sexual objects through which it is gratified, revived, or stimulated. Thus, the break introduced between the fetishism of de Brosses and that of Freud and Marx applies to the transition from the particular to the universal. There is no commodity that does not fall under the commodity form and, therefore, a generalized fetishization (or reification).[5] The same goes for sexuality, especially as soon as this sexuality involves satisfaction through sexual objects that owe their character as objects and as sexual only to their form.

Does Analytic Theory Lead Us to Link Lack to the Sexual?

How do we situate the status of object a in this series of relationships? Both in the commodity form and in sexuality, we are dealing with speaking beings. It is because there are speaking beings that the commodity form makes the desired object shimmer—speaking beings who necessarily lack the object (or the object of objects?) that could fulfill them; it is in the realm of the signifier—of what pretends—that desire, understood as the desire for something other than the desired object, resides. But why? Where does this desire originate? It originates in the body. The speaking being has a body; fundamentally, that is all they have, and this is even the reason why they speak—which means that they speak beyond what they mean, and they also hear something other than what is said. If Freud's *Three Essays on the Theory of Sexuality* is a foundational text for psychoanalysis, it is not so much because of the news that children have sexuality—it was in the air of the time, as Foucault points out in *The History of Sexuality*[6]—but rather because Freud continues, through the example of the body, what he had already envisioned as a program in the *Entwurf*. What is the thesis developed by Freud in the *Entwurf*? I have already hinted at it between the lines: he hypothesizes that there is a "quantity" ($Q\dot{\eta}$, in the text) in the psychic apparatus that cannot be reduced as such, that is never flat, and that never reaches zero. And for what reason? Because only hallucination satisfies it, and in no case an external object or an object of desire. The *Entwurf* is an ethical text (in the sense Lacan gives to this term in the seminar *The Ethics of Psychoanalysis*); it served as a premise for Freud to be able to work as a psychoanalyst.

The Freudian axiom can thus be summarized with the formula "unconscious desire is indestructible." It is indestructible insofar as no object can fulfill it. And conversely: it can destroy any object that claims to fulfill it definitively.

To make one feel that desire is indestructible, Freud gives, as an example of the body that can only be satisfied by itself, the metaphor of the mouth that, if it could, would kiss itself. However, this kissing is impossible. And it is because this kissing is impossible that the desiring subject is "lacking" and must go through the other—the lack is thus central in Freudian theory. If there is this central lack, which Lacan writes as (-φ), that is, this unconscious desire as indestructible ("unconscious" here means that it itself is not conscious and only follows its own will), then something will always be lacking in the speaking being; there is something that they will not find in their body, nor in another body—not in any body, with the paradox that it is only in the body that they can find any pleasure at all, a "pleasure bonus." In other words, there is no being that can fill the lack. Nonetheless, they will spend their life trying to find in the other what they lack (and it is hard to see how they could go about it otherwise); here we have, condensed into one sentence, the fatality that the speaking being encounters. They seek "outside" of this body what the body lacks (Lacan could thus invent the word "extimacy," which is not the opposite of intimacy but rather, intimacy on the outside).

Psychoanalysis thus starts from two intertwined premises: 1) the speaking being is constituted by an irreducible lack; 2) they will seek to fill this irreducible lack in the other. The living being seeks what it lacks in a form (the signifier), and it does so starting with the kiss, which is the gesture that translates desire as it can only be satisfied elsewhere. A gesture as widespread as the kiss—the first and ultimate sign of desire—involves the mouth as a border through which one desires and speaks; language is tied to speech, and everything that passes through this orifice rekindles desire rather than fulfills it. The mouth as an erogenous rim is the place where what will in any case be lacking in desire is expressed. The mouth speaks desire (the signifier) but embraces the lack (what resists the signifier), which is precisely why it cannot kiss itself.

Thus, the relationship established between what is missing (-φ) and what would come to fill this lack bears the mark of a kind of failure. If Lacan makes the sexual act the most well-known form of this failure, it is precisely to diminish the imaginary reference to sexuality, which is supposed to provide the object that man lacks. But is that all? Is sexuality not precisely the symptom of the irreducible lack of being that the sexual claims to remedy?

Sexual fulfillment is supposed to be the beginning of happiness, a necessary but not sufficient cause that must be able to solve two things: first, to satisfy, through pleasure, the most hypostasized form of lack and, second, and above all, to be the condition of love that would supplement the lack that the sexual itself generates, for the sexual drive can only produce lack. Pleasure, sexual desire, love. Fundamentally, what does the speaking being want? It wants to avoid anxiety. We must understand that anxiety is not only a phenomenon but also the formless form of the most paradigmatic disarray of lack. To want to fill the lack means, therefore, to try to avoid the anxiety that this lack produces, and anxiety is like the push to see. It is before the speaking being and has, as a consequence and as a response, desire (notably sexual desire).

And since desire is a manifestation of drives, themselves acephalous—or without specific objects—it can only produce a perpetual lack; note here that love in its variant as the misunderstanding between the sexes is as a response supposed to calm the being in the face of all questioning concerning its lack. Freud always believed that the dreamer essentially wished to sleep: the speaking being primarily wants to calm its lack, to reduce displeasure to the lowest degree; the drive prevents this and restarts the machine. Pleasure is thus the catalyst that intervenes between lack and its fulfillment. The sexual is the horizon of all pleasures,[7] especially as they are disjointed from needs, and sexuality as I have conceived it can only be a norm: in all modern societies, the prohibition of pedophilia, a legal variant of prohibition, has the precise function of constructing a barrier to sexual enjoyment so that normalized sexuality is the standard of a normalization of morals where not everything is permitted (homosexuality, transvestism, masochism, and other sexual practices are no longer forbidden, so they are already framed by the *dispositif* of sexuality). Sexuality as a *dispositif* is not an instance of prohibition but rather of prescription.

As we have seen, lack as such is central because there is no object that can fill it. This is the unveiling of the Freudian project. But with *Three Essays on the Theory of Sexuality*, Freud introduces flesh, which was missing from the expressly flesh-less schemas of the *Entwurf*.[8] Freud's first doctrinal gesture is thus devoid of any sexual relationship; there is only the will to write a libidinal matter, but without qualities. *Three Essays on the Theory of Sexuality* makes the body the place where the possibilities of filling the lack just mentioned unfold, in the form of pleasure (here I am following the text of Milner already cited). Inevitably, Freud links lack to the sexual; it is the body that allows the sexual to have a relationship with lack, and this is the reason that drives J.-C. Milner to speak of "transaction" when it comes to defining the corporeal intermediary through which the sexual introduces a relationship (a sexual relationship) to the central lack of the speaking being. The sexual as such, condemned to inhabit the junction between the least amount of bodily pleasure (displeasure is irreducible: $Q\acute{\eta}$) and the greatest amount of desire that it seeks to fill through the object, thus occupies the function of object a.

Is There a Beyond of the Commodity Form?

For Marx, it is possible to separate exchange value (which produces a "surplus value") from use value. If he was able to advance the idea of a mystification of the commodity form, it is precisely because he intended to demystify it, thereby exposing the mechanisms of the functioning of capitalism. But if we stay close to Milner's text *Le Triple du plaisir*, it goes without saying that these two values co-belong—just like the signifier and the signified—through a hegemony of the signifier. One could easily suppose that Lacan would have adhered to this hypothesis. Opposite this position, Marx advocates the existence of a "complete" man in opposition to the "limited" and "incomplete" man characteristic of the capitalist mode of production and the social constraints it implies—man is limited by exchange value. One would emerge from commodity alienation by recovering what is lost with exchange, by eliminating exchange value as such. But we must not forget that there is in the system described by Marx something that could correspond to an amputated biological function: this is what Marx calls "labor power" (living labor), and which places Marx in the discourse of science through, for example, his multiple references to physiology. Proof of this is the idea of the physiological recovery of the body, which is an integral part of work—and which is called rest (if the boss grants paid vacations to the worker, it is so that he can continue to exploit him as a worker). One could also see in this biological force taken from the worker an equivalent of repression—the only castration that matters, operated by the symbolic order on the living. But Milner, like Freud and contrary to Marx, stipulates that the speaking being has no choice but to be alienated from desire—to be amputated of his labor power—thus leaving the drive permanently unsatisfied. I do not mean by this that the worker must be exploited, but rather that the body, whether it works or not, will be entirely caught in exchange value, which leads Marx to say "man is like a commodity."

But if Marx was right, what would happen to use value? We have said that it is determined by exchange value. But is there not a use as such, a relationship to the worn-out object that would be reduced only to matter? Is there not a relationship to matter, that is, a beyond of exchange value? This is the question we must ask. If reality is necessarily signified and is limited to the commodity form—that is, if there is nothing in reality that escapes the commodity form—then there is no direct relationship to commodities. Yet, there is a relationship to objects, a mediated relationship, but still a relationship. What about it? This relationship becomes a use of objects. What begins as a relationship to the qualities of the object ends up being a material, corporeal relationship to objects: the body seeks and finds satisfaction through an already traced path. If there is satisfaction in use, it is because it satisfies the path already traced in bodily experience; the psychoanalytic notion of fantasy also obeys this principle, and the relationship to the object is built through an "interposed relationship." I am not saying that water does not quench the thirsty or that food does not appease the hungry; I am referring to something beyond fundamental needs (a beyond, of course, difficult to define). The fetish object, that is, the object of desire, marks a break between the "labor power" forever taken from the body—which Freud calls the drive—and exchange value, the qualities of the object that make it desirable. Thus, the body can only recover a small "plus" from the sensible qualities (exchange value) of the object. This is what Lacan calls "surplus jouissance," what owes its existence to the paths traced by the mode of jouissance of the living—a mode always at odds with the objects of desire. And this is why Milner can write,

One understands nothing about *Capital* if one does not discern in it a critical doctrine of qualities. A treatment of qualities that makes them both graspable and compatible with science. The entirety of reality, in the shimmering of diversity, is inscribed in the commodity form. That the commodity is a form means that there is no substance with respect to the commodity, that there is no substantial beyond of use value and exchange value. . . . At the same time, by virtue of the laws of the commodity form, qualities are reduced to exchange value and can be grasped by a general equivalent. In short, commodities are nothing without qualities, but qualities, in the proper sense, only count when abolished and dissolved into an equivalence.[9]

Commodities are nothing outside of qualities, but from the moment they become objects for sale, qualities as such are neutralized and swallowed up by equivalents, starting with that of money. The following hypothesis then imposes itself: these qualities will never satisfy use value, as they will always be out of sync with the use of goods. Just as there is no sexual relationship, meaning no established sexual relationship between the sexes, likewise, there are no natural needs, strictly speaking. But my question remains unanswered: what happens to the distress inherent to the speaking being—a distress that seeks appeasement, from the moment of one's birth to their last breath—themselves deprived of speech but in which the speech of the departing being is omnipresent?

The Exception

It will be understood that use value is closely dependent on exchange value. But at the same time, if there are commodities that circulate, it is because there are buyers, which is to say there is life. Freud calls this life the drive—Lacan, for his part, calls it jouissance. In a certain sense, this jouissance is not commercialized as such; it is not sellable, and it is perfectly useless as such. In this regard, Milner writes,

There are only merchant pleasures. The hypothesis of an irreducible exception remains, a Quality that subsists in the Universe and yet resists the flattening of commercial exchange. One will have recognized labor power and surplus value as the material Grail: that which will always be missing from the most equitable of wages.[10]

In short, surplus value is Marx's object a; labor power and surplus value can never be caught up in the circulation of commodities and the pleasure it entails. Even the most equitable of wages (or the most adequate of sexual relationships) can never pay for the "x," the pound of flesh or the unexchangeable remainder in the supposed equivalence between labor power and exchange value.

The Value of Jouissance

Lacan thus introduces a new dimension of value, which would allow us to see the relationships and differences between use value and exchange value differently. We have seen that there is no beyond the commodity form because this beyond is foreclosed. Everything is absorbed by the commodity form so that there is no need to separate use value from exchange value; in the commercial world, one cannot directly access use value without going through exchange value, in the same way that for Lacan, we do not have a direct relationship to the object because the relationship to the object goes through the signifier. The two values are very different, but they co-belong. We only need to refer to the similarity of the two definitions—one by Marx and the other by Lacan—when defining both the commodity and the signifier. We know all too well Lacan's definition, which I have already quoted: "the signifier is what represents the subject for another signifier." Marx, for his part, writes, "Therefore, when we say that a commodity is in the equivalent form, we express the fact that it is directly exchangeable with other commodities,[11]" or again, "The simple form of value of a commodity is contained in its value or exchange relation with any other kind of commodity."

But there is more: in Marx, the two values are distinguished because something comes between them—namely, the production of the commodity form. In other words, "labor power" comes between them. The commodity form carries within it the trace of the labor form in the form of exchange value (or, more precisely, the gap between the two values reflects the impact of labor power, necessary for the production of objects). Thus, on the one hand, there is a kind of repression of the real thing as such, or of true use, which makes us say that there is not or cannot be, in the circulation of commodities, a direct relationship to them. But, on the other hand, this repressed use value is nothing other than the counterpoint of exchange value, namely the added value thanks to labor power—to human labor—which is itself also somehow repressed; it is not visible in the commodity form, or the final product.

What does it mean that human labor is repressed? It means that one also abstracts from the intrinsic value of the worker, defined, of course, by the worker's working time. And what is precisely repressed—what exchange value does not account for (and what the owner of the means of production extracts without redistributing it)—is the surplus value resulting from the worker's labor (time/labor power/profitability) that the capitalist only remunerates based on a minimum wage that allows him to preserve his being and that of his family as constituting a future reservoir of workers. Strictly speaking, the more time a worker takes to make a commodity, the more expensive that commodity should be, since one pays for the strength used up by the manufacturing. It goes without saying that in the valorization of two commodities through exchange value, there are two terms that are repressed, if not crushed: use value as such and the labor power employed to create the differential between the natural value of the object and its exchange value. Surplus value is the added value obtained by this differential, surplus value that would maintain a close relationship with Lacan's notion of "surplus jouissance"; this latter concept is only understood if it is opposed to that of jouissance.

In this regard, this statement by Milner in another jointly authored work should enlighten us:

If you take the first book of *Capital*, which is the foundational book, value represents what there is of labor power in each object bearing value, but it can only represent it in a commercial exchange, that is, for another value. Now, labor power is simply the subject. This is the name Marx gives to the subject. Therefore, the Marxist formula of the structure of exchange and the Lacanian formula of the signifier overlap in an extremely precise way. . . . Suppose that Lacan did not immediately think of Marx. It is known that, with him, formulas are stated in the dimension of haste; the subsequent movement of interpretation of the formula somehow legitimizes the formula itself. It is thus after the fact that the notion of 'surplus jouissance', explicitly modeled on the notion of surplus value, will validate the possible analogy between the definition of the signifier and Marx's definition of value.[12]

In this statement, we have several formulations that fit together. On the one hand, there is the very production of value generated by the differentials between natural value and added value through the relation of commodities; on the other hand, it appears that this added value is the imprint left by labor power, which, as we have seen, does not appear as such, just like the natural value of the object (use value). Finally, the notion of surplus value can be nothing other than the value extracted from labor power, since the object is nothing other than the support of a surplus that exceeds it.

Lacan and Marx

When Lacan discusses the relationship between use value and exchange value in his seminar *La logique du fantasme*, he mentions a curious formula from Feuerbach, the author of *Philosophical Manifestos*: "The object of man is nothing other than his essence taken as an object. The object also to which a subject relates, by essence and necessarily, is nothing other than the subject's own essence, non-objectified."[13] This formula seems, at first glance, quite obscure. What is the essence of the subject? Something that is neither the individual nor the object. Feuerbach gives us a new version of the object (let's be clear: Lacan also gives us a new version of the object), a version that is neither the object nor the individual (the man). Under Lacan's formulation, 1) man, the speaking being, has an object; 2) this object is his own essence, which means that it is not the object as such that is his essence (one could say that, since the seminar on *Anxiety*, it is also his libidinal reserve); 3) this object is his essence transformed into an object that is his true object (the starting point of the formula is "the object of man") and not the objects to which man "relates"; 4) the essence of man is not objectified: it remains "non-objectified," as it would be in the nature of essence to remain without "objectal" attributes, or without objectal qualities.

The essence of the speaking being is his own castration—namely, that as a speaking being, he is spoken more than he speaks, and castration is his "original castration." He is spoken by language in what is irreducible to language—namely, the drive, according to Freud and jouissance, according to Lacan. Furthermore, the idea of a libidinal reserve is interesting insofar as it makes the drive positive, instead of considering it as a void, a deficit, or a lack. The essence of man—in other words, the object of man, for these two notions are equivalent—is what is irreducible to exchange. Thus, we have a series of irreducibles: the drive, jouissance, labor power, and the object a.

Let us return to Lacan and to what he specifies in his seminar *La logique du fantasme*:

> We saw earlier that it is from the false identification of exchange value with use value that the foundation of the commodity-object results. One can even say more—that it takes capitalism for this thing, which predates it by far, to be revealed. Similarly, at the principle of value at the level of the unconscious, there is something that takes the place of exchange value. . . . We will call it . . . the value of jouissance.[14]

What is at stake is therefore a "false identification" where the commodity circulates thanks to an unconscious value ("the value at the level of the unconscious") which gives the "true" value to exchange value and certainly does not coincide with use value. We thus recognize Lacan's formulation regarding "the object of man," namely his essence: "the value at the level of the unconscious." This is why Lacan advances the idea that what takes the place of the rules of the elementary structures of kinship and alliance is an unconscious value, in the sense of the Freudian unconscious, which certainly differs from the rules of alliance that Lévi-Strauss describes as being "unconscious." Why? Because the rules derive their power from a prohibition, a deprivation, or a gap between the desired object and the enjoyed object; it is in this gap, in this *Spaltung*, that the object a is lodged.

Let us once again highlight what Lacan implies in his statement: 1) there are two different values: exchange value and use value; 2) These two values are equated, mainly because they are not equal; 3) This equalization is obtained through a third value: the value of jouissance. Castration and repression are inherent to the unconscious and limit the series of imaginary objects, whether it be the scybalum or the penis. This is what Lacan demonstrates when he asserts that it would be very evocative to imagine the sex of a bull to get an idea of the phallus:

> If there is something that gives a clear idea of use value, it is what one does when bringing in a bull for a certain number of mounts. It is peculiar that no one has imagined inscribing the elementary structures of kinship [cf. Lévi-Strauss] in this circulation of the all-powerful phallus. . . . Curiously, it is we [the analysts] who discover that this phallic value is represented by the woman. . . . In other words, here is something reversed. It is no longer the sex of our bull, use value, that will serve this kind of circulation [use value] established in the sexual order; it is the woman, inasmuch as she herself has, on this occasion, become the place of transfer of the value subtracted at the level of use value [thus, exchange value], in the form of the object of jouissance.[15]

In a sort of twist, what is subtracted at the level of use value (pure jouissance of the sexual organ, inconceivable as such and especially nonexchangeable) is reversed (in the sense of both a twist and the transfer of a substance) onto the woman taken as an object. This could explain Feuerbach's formula: "The object of man is nothing other than his essence taken as an object." The object of man's desire (the woman) is the essence of man (his phallus/his castration) taken as the object of desire—a phallic circulation of women taken as exchange value. But if these are objects of exchange, it is because they are not, strictly speaking, the objects of man. This value, once it is subtracted from use value (impossible auto-erotism), is transferred onto the woman, and this transfer is realized in the form of an object of desire. Under these conditions, the object a is a "negative quality,"[16] absolute proof of the "negative incidence"[17] of desire.

Notes

1 Iacono A., *Le fétichisme dans l'amour*, Payot, Paris, 2001.
2 Marx K., *Capital: A Critique of Political Economy*, Volume 1, Reprint edition, Penguin Classics, London, 1992.
3 Descola, P., *Par-delà nature et culture*, Gallimard, Paris, 2005.
4 Iacono A., *Fétichisme, Histoire d'un concept*, PUF, Paris, 1992, p. 102.
5 Lucaks G., *History & Class Consciousness*, Merlin Press, 1967.
6 Foucault M., *The History of Sexuality*, Pantheon Books, New York, 1978.
7 Milner J.-C., *Le triple du plaisir*, Verdier, Paris, 1997, p. 65.
8 Freud S., "Project for a scientific psychology", in *The Revised Standard Edition of the Complete Psychological Works of Sigmund Freud*, Volume I, Revised édition, translated by James Strachey and Mark Solms, Rowman & Littlefield, London, 2024.
9 Milner J.-C., *Triple du plaisir*, Verdier, Paris, p. 75–76.
10 Milner J.-C., *Triple du plaisir*, Verdier, Paris, p. 76–77.
11 Marx K., *Capital: A Critique of Political Economy*, Volume 1, Reprint edition, Penguin Classics, London, 1992, p. 52.
12 Milner J.-C., *Clartés de tout*, Verdier, Paris, 2011, p. 89.
13 Lacan J., *La logique du fantasme*, Seuil, Paris, 2023, p. 265 (my translation).
14 Lacan J., *La logique du fantasme*, Seuil, Paris, 2023, p. 266–267.
15 Lacan J., *La logique du fantasme*, Seuil, Paris, 2023, p. 268.
16 According to Jean-Claude Milner (personal communication).
17 Lacan J., "The youth of gide, or the letter and desire", in *Ecrits*, W. W. Norton & Company, 2006, p. 635.

Conclusion

The hypotheses that led me to reconstruct the notion of object a throughout this book were as follows: the concept of object a can be derived from two types of definitions—a negative definition and a positive definition. The first is relatively simple to formulate and follows from Lacan's hypothesis of the primacy of the symbolic, a hypothesis that, I would say, is more than verified: the symbolic annihilates things as they are by replacing them with a signifying system ("killing of the thing"), so object a can only be a consequence of this indirect relationship with the world.

Regarding the positive definition of object a, it is quite a different matter. It takes root, in my view, at the level of the imaginary register and appears to Lacan in the form of the gaze. What is it about? I have given particular importance to the deployment of an initial intuition in Lacan—chronologically speaking initial, that is—namely, the theory of the "mirror stage." It seems essential to me for several reasons. I was able to reconstruct the development of this initial theory, particularly as it becomes more complex as Lacan's work progresses, culminating in the production of the "optical schema," a kind of substitute, in the psychoanalyst's own words, for the mirror stage. This optical schema is presented during Lacan's first published seminar, but it too becomes more complex in turn. This evolution seems to reach its peak during the seminar *Angoisse* ("anxiety"), where Lacan gives crucial importance to the famous gesture of the child's head "turning," which I interpreted as the existence of joint attention, the culmination of the child's incorporation of the symbolic.

We thus have three elements that emerge from this major moment: a) the image of one's own body (or that of the other), which Lacan writes as "i(a)"; b) the emergence of an ideal point, linked to this mediating other, which Lacan calls the ego ideal and writes as "I(A)"; and, finally, (c) what results from the gap between the image of oneself and this kind of necessarily external point from which the desiring subject sees themselves living. This division, this "split," translates into the "object a function." If object a is so important to Lacan, it is because it condenses—particularly through the gaze and the voice—what forever separates the divided being and constitutes a kind of definitive stability. It is through the gesture of the head's nutation, which Lacan repeatedly returns to in the early 1960s in his article

DOI: 10.4324/9781003614203-8

"Remarks on Daniel Lagache's Presentation," culminating in the publication of the *Écrits* in 1966 ("On My Antecedents"), that the psychoanalyst can articulate and definitively define the paradigmatic status of object a. This moment of turning is also the turning point of my book; I propose that it is through this essential exchange with the other—this moment of sharing that occurs through the gaze—that we can locate, in the same movement, this dual relationship to the other. This other gives consistency (in the sense of mediation) to the image, or to the ego, but it also relativizes (by diminishing it) the importance of this image.

One may rightfully wonder why Lacan had not spoken about the object a before this date (i.e., the early 1960s). I'll restate my hypothesis in order to insist: it is through this key moment of incorporating the symbolic world that Lacan arrives at the concept of the object of objects. It is through the construction of the gaze and its differentiation from vision that he is able to give body to this entirely drive-based object. It is this symbolic instance of the other that, on the one hand, allows the living being to anchor its drive to the objects of the shareable world and, on the other hand, makes it as dissatisfied as possible because this symbolic regime inevitably produces a lack that can only be remedied through the other.

Why would the gaze object be the paradigm of object a? The gaze, as we have seen, is the support of a mediation with the other, which differentiates it from the vision of the first weeks of the child's life. What the child sees is unrelated to the fact that it is the gaze of the other that leads them there; desire is the desire of the other, regardless of the object of this desire. The gaze of the other—punctual and evanescent in that it is repressed as such, because it is diverted to an external object—is the Alpha and Omega of the relationship with the world. If this gaze initiates an interest in the world—the movement toward the other and toward oneself—it is also, for Lacan, the moment of a fall, of turning toward what it is in this other that pushes us to see. One's own self, insofar as it is an image, only makes sense because, without the gaze of this other who continues to play within us, it would be emptied of its meaning.

Index

For Product Safety Concerns and Information please contact our EU
representative GPSR@taylorandfrancis.com
Taylor & Francis Verlag GmbH, Kaufingerstraße 24, 80331 München, Germany